ECONOMIC ISSUES, PROBLEMS AND PERSPECTIVES

OPENING VIEWS AGAINST THE CLOSURE OF THE WORLD

Economic Issues, Problems and Perspectives

Additional books in this series can be found on Nova's website under the Series tab.

Additional e-books in this series can be found on Nova's website under the e-book tab.

ECONOMIC ISSUES, PROBLEMS AND PERSPECTIVES

OPENING VIEWS AGAINST THE CLOSURE OF THE WORLD

PETER HERRMANN

nova publishers
New York

Library of Congress Cataloging-in-Publication Data

ISBN: 978-1-63484-090-3

Published by Nova Science Publishers, Inc. † New York

CONTENTS

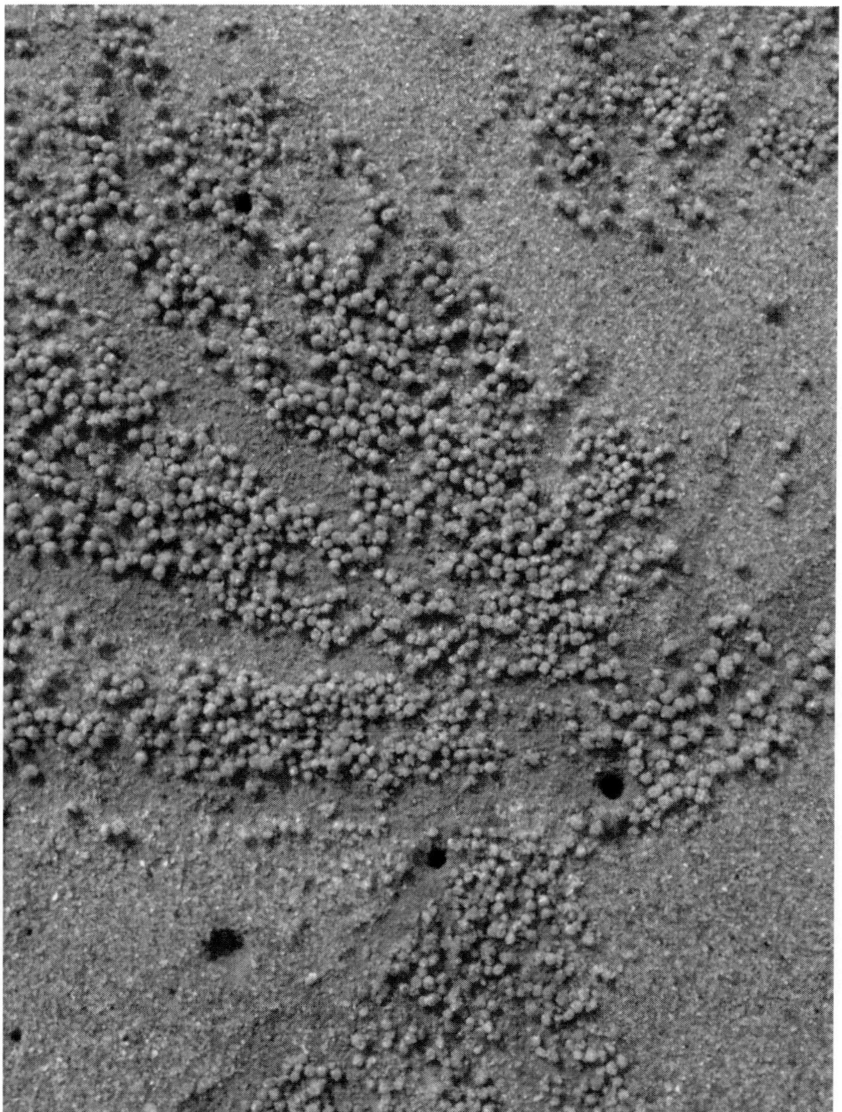

DEDICATION

Of course, life is complex and a political dedication is always in danger of falling short, not sufficiently reflecting the actual complexities.

Of course, life is full of contradictions and a political dedication is always in danger of falling short, not sufficiently reflecting these contradictions.

Just those days when I had been compiling the texts for this edition, I had been interrupted by the news of the massacre in Paris. Actually at the very moment when the massacre in Paris happened against Charlie Hebdo, against the values which emerged with the elevation of the halved modernity: the modernity of the bourgeoisie and the specifically educated citoyenitée, I had been working in the library of *l'école française de Rome,* in the Palazzo Farnese – disconnected, without news from the world outside, and only hearing in the evening about what happened: the massacre that killed too many people, that left too many behind – with their grief, their inability to understand, their anger … – with our grief, our inability to understand, our anger …

Still, much needs to be said, requires debates, requires … just one commitment of all of us. To speak out loud – and to claim this elementary right.

[1]

[1]http://assets.nydailynews.com/polopoly_fs/1.2068947!/img/httpImage/image.jpg_gen/derivatives/article_970/charlie-hebdo.jpg - 09.01.15

About the Author

Prof. Dr. Peter Herrmann

Rome, Italy
E-mail: herrmann@esosc.eu
skype: peteresosc
QQ: 2738027550
http://williamthompsonucc.wordpress.com

Peter Herrmann - Dr. Phil. (Bremen, Germany). Studies in Sociology (Bielefeld, Germany), Economics (Hamburg, Germany), Political Science (Leipzig, Germany) and Social Policy and Philosophy (Bremen, Germany).

Since 2013 living in Rome, Italy and working globally as social philosopher. He is also adjunct professor at the University of Eastern Finland (UEF), Department of Social Sciences (Kuopio, Finland), honorary associate professor at Corvinus University in Budapest, Faculty of Economics, Department of World Economy.

Dr. Herrmann had been teaching at several Third Level Institutions across the EU; currently correspondent to the Max Planck Institute for Foreign and International Social Law (Munich, Germany). He holds position as for instance that of a senior advisor to the European Foundation on Social Quality (The Hague, Netherlands), member of the Advisory Board of EURISPES – Istituto di Studi Politici, Economici e Sociali, Rome, member of the Scientific Board and its coordination committee of ATTAC – Association pour la taxation des transactions financières pour l'aide aux citoyens, Associate Member of the Eurasian Center for Big History and System Forecasting, Lomonosow Moscow State University, Russia. He held various positions as visiting professor at different universities within ad outside of the EU. He also had been research fellow at National Taiwan University, Taipei; The Cairns Institute, James Cook University, Australia; Visiting Scholar at Orta Dogu Teknik Üniversitesi (ODTU), Ankara, Turkey; Visiting Scholar at the Max-Planck-Institute für Sozialrecht und Sozialpolitik, Munich, Germany.

Dr. Herrmann started his work in researching European Social Policy and in particular the role of NGOs. His main interest shifted over the last years towards developing the Social Quality Approach further, looking in particular into the meaning of economic questions and questions of law. He linked this with questions on the development of state analysis and the question of social services. On both topics he published widely.

Member of several editorial boards; editor of the book series Applied Social Studies – Recent Developments, International and Comparative Perspectives (New York, USA) and Studies in Comparative Pedagogies and International Social Work and Social Policy (Bremen, Germany) [until 2015], now changed to Studies in Global Social Policy and Practice (New York, USA/Oxford, UK); peer-reviewing for several journals in the social area and book series.

PREFACE

OUTLINING THE FIELD OF SEARCH

The contributions collected in this volume are all centred around challenges we face globally – saying globally means that they such perspective has to be taken seriously by looking at the global system not in terms of division of labour and relation between national and regional entitites but in terms of a Unitarian common socio-natural space. Too often social science remains explicitly limited by understanding the process of globalisation as a matter of (i) maintaining the old developmentalist perspective, presuming the superiority of what is today called global north or (ii) as suspicious, i.e., defending in one way or another indigeneity. A possible further move consists in (iii) claiming some form of merger, the *caminare insieme,* for which the present pope can claim some fame. However, by maintaining the two other approaches, this is reduced on some moral statement, translated into demanding collective rationality against greed and the appeal to mercy, facing the invisible hand with the negative effects of pure individualism. We face a huge gap here and there when it comes to developing an understanding that goes fundamentally further, actually seriously discussing the autochthonous mindsets. Saying this, it is also necessary to remind us that these concepts are less autochthonous than often assumed. Using a generous approach, human rights may be dated back to the *Declaration of Man and of the Citizen* from 1789, in a narrow way they should be linked to the *Universal Declaration of Human Rights* from 1948 where they had been codified and universalised; the modern nation state is usually seen in connection with the Westphalian Peace Treaty from 1648, and on the other hand the social question in its current form is commonly dated back to the times of industrialisation with its beginning in the middle of the 1700s – with this we follow Robert Castel's argument that asking the social question had been the answer on the dissolution of primary social relationships which provided immediate securitisation *(see Castel, 1995).* History calls for caution – and though I do not dare to claim that I made a radical rupture in thinking, I tried. And I also tried to give space for questions instead of hastily coming up with answers.

One of the major recurring problems in social science is the understanding of society as complex entity versus an understanding of society as amalgamation of subsystems, emerging from rational individuals, pursuing their own gains. A particularly important point in this debate is concerned with 'localising the economy', which of course entails the definition of the economy or economic activities. This is a matter that plays a role within societies and it is of equal importance when it comes to developmental issues on a global scale. For the latter we may look at the emergence of the developmental question, reaching from the simple *'we know what is good for you'* of harsh colonialism to the *'you can see what is good for you'* as Rostowian take, suggesting a universal path of development to again another notion suggesting *'we will strive for what is good for all of us'* as shorthand for the strategy of the Millennium Developmental Goals to a another new strategy of *'we have to define what is good for us'* as reflected in the Post-2015 Development Agenda. All these approaches have one fundamental issue in common: an apparent self-evident meaning and knowledge of the 'social and its values', of course most pronouncedly brought forward by the claim of natural rights – unquestioned and unquestionable as the need of heart-beat as condition for human life.

Sure, it may be questioned if (and if so to which extent) these outlooks are fundamentally differing from each other. Although there are surely differences between them, it is equally clear that the underlying 'model' is that of a capitalist mode of production, shaped as capitalocene. It also refers to a very specific capitalist anthropology as it had been outlined by Herbert Marcuse *(see Marcuse, 1966: CD 2: track 1: 2.45 min)*

It seems that the new orientation, i.e., the orientation of the Post-2015 Development Agenda, is about a broader consultation – expressing the general shift to what is called governance – and the orientation on transforming the economy, namely orienting on jobs and growth which had not been expressed with the same clarity in the debate on the MDGs. The way in which 'sustainability' is emphasised appears also to be new.

The background of such change is wide-ranging, not least in addressing the question of 'localising the economic sphere'. Des Gasper proposes the following ordering:

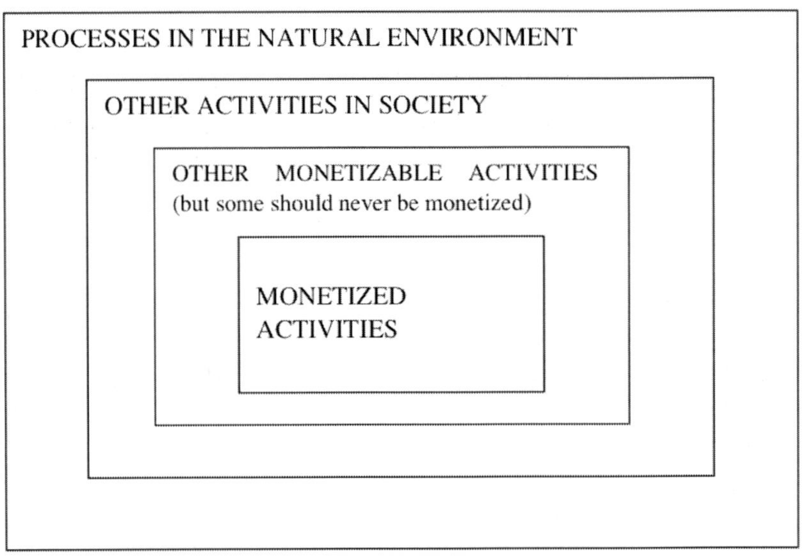

(Gasper, 2010: 10; with reference to Gasper, 2004).

Though this is a valuable heuristic presentation some hesitation remains in accepting it, suggesting that a 'new strategy' may require something thety allows going further.

First: Seeing the current system as centred around monetised activities is one aspect; at the same time we see a pattern that goes far beyond centring – actually the monetised system is to some extent 'external', or better to say, the other systems are externalised. In simple terms we are dealing with the question of externalising costs, subsequently suggesting that procedures as full budgeting etc. are conceptually impossible. However, we face the question if full budgeting and similar mechanisms can in actual fact mean the strengthening the process of commodification and monetisation by drawing more elements into this 'economist core'. The following quote from another context does also apply here: 'When authors state that 'economic facts' are 'embedded' in the social … they suppose that there is something we can identify as 'economic' which at the same time can be distinguished from the 'social' … In a way, they are themselves drawing the boundary they are trying to question.' (This Saint-Jean, 2005: 318f., translation P.H.)

The first 'complementing modification' to Gasper's presentation suggests turning it around, having the monetised activities as 'ring', strangulating the others. We can also reformulate this, asking if we should talk about cost or if it is more important to think about the production of things, relations and processes. From here we can move on, inquiring about the standard that provides the framework for such definition. The challenge is to work along the line of distinct ontological levels.

A second 'complementing modification' is then about taking the monetised activities out of the immediate system, presenting them as hegemon. With this the entire eco-sociability is also defined without, however, considering it directly as part of the equation (perhaps the term antropocene can be usefully applied here too).

This is not a purely academic question but as well important as it allows us to approach an issue which is frequently left out of considerations, as it seems to be too difficult for approaches that are strictly socio- and political-economic (instead, we leave 'decisions' to moralists and ethicists …, and their appeals). Too often economics, reduces by and large, its own realm – and society at large – on dealing with commodities and their exchange within a rationalist, contractualist framework: on the one hand this is exclusive as nothing else is considered within this model; and it is on the other hand inclusive as the entire eco-social system is following these rules. And indeed, we can use the regulationist theory to develop this further: the core concepts of accumulation regime and mode of regulation are reflected in specific living regimes and modes of life. It is not simply about basis-superstructure relations though this is of course also a relevant question. However, we have to develop further that certain modes of production with their accumulation regimes 'produce' certain ways of consumption – the latter understood in a broad way and as such also including time-consumption, certain life styles etc.. Fordism is surely an excellent example as mass consumption had been inherent part, and the same applies for the changed patterns of income distribution. We have to emphasis that Fordism had not been just about mass-production and mass-consumption; instead, it established an entire 'way of life' and meant furthermore an entirely different way of shaping society. In other words it is about the entirety of producing society and producing society's understanding of space and time. Fordism is – somewhat – past; however, talking today about post-Fordism seems to be a way of avoiding today's real questions about the new understanding of the social fabric, which is now surely a global one. Although we find some notions of an 'imperial mode of life' becoming popular *(see e.g., Brand/Wissen, 2012),* this fails to address the fact that we are actually dealing with a fundamentally 'economic' question of production, and not with a simple 'imperialist move' forcing Coke® into every hut on the globe while people are looking through the standardised Windows® on the computer screen. We have to redefine economy and economics in order to understand the far-reaching changes that are linked to the question of understanding non-capitalist pathways as alternatives.

This raises another point. Taking again a quote from the very insightful work of Des Gasper we see that 'the identities which 'individuals' declare or compose are built from socially constructed elements; ... the construction of community identities at various levels was central in anti-colonial struggles for political freedoms, and is likely to be equally central in other and future struggles ...' (Gasper, 2009: 291)

Thus we arrive at another point when it comes to reconsidering globalisation beyond global capitalism. A very common reference is made to the 'three generations' of human rights, as outlined by Karel Vasak *(see Vasak, 1977).* Such classification does not provide much space for the rights of self-determination beyond or deeper than the level of defending freedoms on the level of self-determination, i.e., it does not provide any rights dealing with the conditions of self-determination: the 'what, for what and how to produce'.

Human Rights in their current version are taking the capitalist mode of production for granted and unquestionable as 'global solution'. Looking for a New Style of Development *(see Dubois/Lasida, 2010)* may then already look suspicious and evoke rejection. In more favourable interpretations, such suggestions may be seen as matter of utopian dreams. However, the problem is that they are actually utopian dreams as long as *the conditions that would allow their wider realisation* remain underdeveloped – in (human rights) law, in real economy and in economics alike. And these conditions are in fact not so much about lacking resources and means of production for further socialisation, but about the control over the means of production, bringing us indeed back to the question of hegemony. The other way round, any emancipative counter-hegemony has to secure fully establishing the character of work/labour as social movement *(see page 176).* – There are surely major challenges ahead in addressing the core limitations which are not least result of Western-capitalist hegemony, pervasively perverting too often also the search for alternatives.

Redundancies in the present collection could not be avoided – but they may also be helpful for the reader. On the one hand it is easily possible to read the contributions individually, which means also: to read one without the others. On the other hand, reading all of them allows to clearly understand the different angles for which some core elements – especially of social quality thinking – are needed, and where the specific application actually gives each of them a slightly different meaning, emphasising one aspect, sidelining another. At the end, taken together, it is about applying the relational approach which is in itself a matter of relationality.

REFERENCES

Brand, Ulrich/Wissen, Markus, 2012: Global Environmental Politics and the Imperial Mode of Living: Articulations of State–Capital Relations in the Multiple Crisis, Globalizations, 9:4, 547-560; http://dx.doi.org/10.1080/14747731.2012.699928.

Castel, Robert, 1995: Les Métamorphoses de la Question Sociale. Une Chronique du Salariat; Paris: Libraire Arthème Fayard.

Dubois, Jean-Luc/Lasida, Elena, 2010: A new Style of Development to Deal with the Current Crisis: Solidarity-based Economy, Collective Capability and Sustainable Human Development: in: Markets, governance and human development; numéro coordonné par

Anand, P.B./Gasper, Des/Teschl, Miriam; revue de philosophie économique, 11/1; Association de philosophie économique (ed.): 35-56.

Gasper, Des, 2004: The Ethics of Development: From Economism to Human Development, Edinburgh University Press, Edinburgh.

Gasper, Des, 2009: From Valued Freedoms, to Polities and Markets the Capability Approach in Policy Practice; in: Revue Tiers monde, N° 198 - Avril-Juin 2009: 285-302.

Gasper, Des, 2010: Goods and persons, reasons and responsibilities; International Journal of Social Economics, Vol. 34 No. 1/2, 2007; Emerald Group Publishing Limited: 6-18; DOI 10.1108/03068290710723336.

Marcuse, Herbert, 1966: Der Mensch in einer sozialisierten Welt. Aufnahme: 03.10.1966, BR Technik: Schmitt Laufzeit: 47:13; CD 2: track 1: 2.45 min; from: Der Mensch in einer sozialisierten Welt. Originalvorträge von Herbert Marcuse. Autor: Herbert Marcuse. Sprecher: Herbert Marcuse. Aus der Reihe: O-Ton-Wissenschaft. Thema: Soziologie, Wissenschaft. 4 CDs - ca. 200 Minuten.

This Saint-Jean, Isabelle, 2005: Peut-on définir la sociologie économique?, in: Philippe Steiner and Isabelle This Saint-Jean (eds.): Sociologies Économiques. L'Année sociologique 55 (2005); http://www.cairn.info/revue-l-annee-sociologique-2005-2-page-307.htm - 09/09/2014; DOI: 10.3917/anso.052.0307 http://www.cairn.info/load_pdf.php?ID_ARTICLE=ANSO_052_0307 - 01/01/15: 307 – 326.

Vasak, Karel, 1977: A 30-Year Struggle. The Sustained Efforts to Give Force of Law to the Universal Declaration of Human Rights; in: The UNESCO Courier. A Window open on the World; Paris: UNESCO: 30/11: 29/32 - http://unesdoc.unesco.org/images/0007/000748/074816eo.pdf ; 05/11/14.

ACKNOWLEDGMENTS

The presentation at hand is a collection of revised conference-papers and original contributions. Some had been already published in this or a different form as working papers. There are many people with whom I discussed relevant matters, and I hope there are many people with whom I can discuss matters in the future. There are also many people and institutions to whom I owe thanks. Not all can be mentioned – and I will limit explicit thanks to the following: All Russian Centre of Living Standards, namely Vyacheslav Bobkov; Balassi Intézet, Budapest; Centro de Investigaciones de Política Internacional, Havana; Department of World Economy at the Faculty of Economics at the Corvinus University, Budapest; Eurasian Center for Big History & System Forecasting Center, namely Andrey Korotayev and Leonid Grinin; Magyar Tudományos Akadémia, Társadalomtudományi Kutatóközpont and especially Bódi Ferenc and Róbert Péter; the University of Eastern Finland (UEF), Department of Social Sciences, namely Juhani Laurinkari and Veli-Matti Poutanen; and not least the Zhejiang University, Hangzhou, namely Ka Lin. I want to extend my thanks to the following colleagues and friends: Rudolph Bauer, Paul Boccara, Catherine Mills, Yves Dimicoli, Jean-Luc Dubois, Marica Frangakis, Frieder-Otto Wolf and not least Ferge Zsuzsa and John Veit-Wilson. With all of them I have had the privilege of many encouraging discussions over the years and of enyoing their friendship.

****

I am grateful for financial support from the School of Public Affairs, Dept. of Social Security and Risk Management at Zhejiang University, Hangzhou

and

Bangor College CSUFT, Changsha, Hunan,
both in the PR China. The generosity allowed me to work on the final editing.

Part I, Scene I: Night
In a high-vaulted Gothic chamber, Faust, in a chair, at his desk, restless

Faust:
What do you say to me, bare grinning skull
(35)

Chapter 1

RESEARCH ON DEMAND ACADEMICS BETWEEN SELF-CONSCIOUSNESS AND SELF-CHASTISEMENT

ZUSAMMENFASSUNG

Forschung on demand wird oft als Fremdbestimmung, z.B. im Rahmen von Auftragsforschung, verstanden. Dies ist sicherlich eine Bedrohung. Dagegen steht die Forderung nach Eigenverantwortung.

Im vorgesehenen Beitrag soll aber auf 3 Punkte hingewiesen werden, die nur zu leicht vergessen werden: zusammenfassen lassen sich diese Bereiche unter den Stichworten Elfenbeinturm, Überspezialisierung und mangelnde interne und externe Diskursfähigkeit.

1) Wissenschaft(ler) haben gerade in Eigenverantwortung zu der heutigen Form von Fremdbestimmung beigetragen – Stichwort: 'Elfenbeinturm'
2) Wissenschaft(ler) haben sich gerade in Eigenverantwortung dadurch abgeschottet, dass sie sich immer stärker diszipliniert hat/haben – Stichwort: 'Überspezialisierung' und 'Professionalisierung'
3) Wissenschaft(ler) haben gerade in Eigenverantwortung verpasst und verpassen es noch heute, sich auf die tatsächlichen Herausforderungen einzustellen, begnügen sich oft mit einer Defensivhaltung kleiner Prinzregentenschaften anstatt aktiv die Fähigkeit zu gesellschaftlicher Praxis unter Beweis zu stellen – Stichwort: 'mangelnde interne und externe Diskursfähigkeit'

Freilich hängen die 3 Bereiche eng zusammen. Um dies nach deren kurzer Skizzierung verständlich zu machen, wird auf die schon früh, nicht zuletzt in der Aufklärung, zu findende Verankerung des individualistischen Denkens eingegangen.

Gibt es da einen Ausweg?

Introduction

Courage is the first step to anything great.
(Goethe)

Currently we find frequently discussions highlighting facts around the alienation of scientific work. Actually these debates are rather frequent, though they may take different forms: rights to self-determination are posed against determination by profitability; bureaucratic influence and quests for efficiency are criticised as matter of irrelevance and incompetence; but we find also the strive for 'relevance', calling for responsibility as matter of leaving the 'ivory tower' of pure reason, asking for relevance of research for communities (e.g., Greenhalgh 2015). Without doubt, there are important issues linked to such catchwords. However, the present contribution argues that we find also tendencies that are inherent in the historical foundation of science, i.e., the embeddedness of the development of scientific thinking in wider socio-ideological developments, leading to a (potential) self-restraint.

Even if I suppose that Adam Smith is to large extent one of the most problematic precursors of political economy, serving rightly or wrongly as reference for today's harsh capitalist oppressive structures of neo-liberalism, I will make a positive reference to his work. And although I think many of contemporary critical approaches to education fall short due to their fundamentally idealist foundation, I will make frequent reference to Friedrich von Schiller and his surely idealist approach to questions of education, again taking this orientation not least as positive point of reference. Different considerations stand behind this reasoning. *First,* it is because the sections I will refer to are simply thoughtful and thought-provoking. It is about phrases and sentences that are – not least when read in isolation – so appealing also for us today. They come across as timeless wisdom. *Second,* I make this reference also in order to show that such supposed 'eternal wisdom' is highly problematic. *Third,* then, this reference is made in order to approach issues that are today discussed in such superfluous, shallow way, prevalent for a long time; actually I could have gone much further back in looking for sources – not doing so is due to the fact that I want to ventilate some thoughts that are more specifically linked to today's issues. My thesis is that the origin of many problems we discuss today as matter of freedom of science and the lack of it have to be understood as deeply rooted in the emerging 'modern', 'capitalist' society. Before looking at the classics, some other remarks may introduce us into the topic.

We still have some general issues as underlying reference – with some justification we can speak of an anthropological strand of the argument. But even these have to be related to historically more specific issues. As such they find their very specific characterisation by the development of the productive forces. This means, *fourth,* that the reference to the development of the productive forces allows developing a sound analytical perspective, not reducing the assessment of current research matters and the development of Third-Level-Systems on interpreting it as outcome of the hegemonic tightening of individual capitalists and corporations as backers jockeys and their power-driven finish on the home stretch of casino capitalism. Nor will it be sufficient to reduce the assessment of current developments by making reference to catch-all slogans like neo-liberalism, globalisation and the like. This does not suggest that the mainstream arguments are completely irrelevant. Actually I am far from suggesting that there are no real threats from a bureaucratic hegemonic class.

Nevertheless, I want to highlight some historical pathways that show that science itself is captured by some inherent contradictions, thus inclined to develop vulnerability, or even inherently driving towards something that we tentatively may call self-inflicted alienation from scientific aims.

SCIENCE AND AIMS OF SCIENTIFIC WORK

On this occasion only a short look will do suffice, suggesting the following points as central characteristics.

The point of reference can be seen as outcome and specification of wider social and societal practice. In the first realm – as social practice – we are dealing with the social as process of relational appropriation. We are facing an institutional setting that serves as frame for the current societal practice. It emerges as distinct environment which has to be taken into account in its own right.

As much as we can say that social actors – or even human beings – are in general always also part of their own environment, we can see this as being especially true for the relationship of science as social action and the institutionalised system of science. In this light the scientific community may be seen as intersection between different relevant areas. This implies that science is closely linked to reality – as abstract as it may appear, science and scientific work are always as well an answer to existing questions, and in this way 'research on demand' is defined by the complex socio-economic, socio-technical, socio-political, socio-natural realities (and their interwoven character).

Such demand emerges from the following points (though they are only analytically separable). The *first* is a matter of immediate soci(et)al practice – the relationship between human being and environment. The *second* is a matter of the mediated practice – again a matter of the relationship between human being and environment, but now in terms of complex and coordinated practice between human beings. The *third* is a matter of human beings and environment, now the 'we' being replaced by a socially differentiated and structured system of 'we' and 'they', relating to the environment: 'we' as society at large, 'they' as scientific community and environment. The *fourth* is a matter of a by and large self-reflexive scientific community, in the extreme cases founding its work on the idea of l'art pour l'art. And of course, looking in particular at the third point we have to acknowledge that the 'we' is not an abstract entity but a historically defined entity of differentiated relationships as they emerge from the development of the productive forces. On the other hand, dealing with science – as *'knowledge (of something) acquired by study,' (http://www.etymonline.com/index.php?allowed_in_frame=0&search=science&searchmode=none - 28/09/2011 8:08 a.m.)* – means to deal inherently with some form of abstraction. This is applicable in two respects: it is knowledge acquired by way of a very specific process of appropriation, i.e., study, which entails some form of distancing from immediate practice. And it is an abstraction in terms of knowledge as something that can be stored and combined in its own terms – with all the social, temporal and spatial implications. To be sure, this is not a matter of 'complete independence', let alone a matter of any mystical character of knowledge.

With this 'distancing', science and knowledge moves into a new realm of relationships, heavily determined by 'inherent interests'. Reflexive, self-satisfying knowledge is one dimension; another dimension is that knowledge can now be combined with different interests. This distancing has to be seen as inherent part of the process of civilisation. Two dimensions are of interest.

The one is occupied by the totality as *soci(et)al practice based on real utopia.* It deals with spaces of possibilities and opportunities as they had been outlined elsewhere (see Herrmann, 2010; with reference to Bloch, 1959). It is distancing in the sense which Schiller presents in the following words:

> But why call it mere game, when we consider that in every condition of humanity it is precisely play, and play alone, that makes man complete and displays at once is twofold nature? What you call limitation, according to your conception of the matter, I call extension according to mine … (Schiller, 1794: 79)

The other – paradoxically – is a matter of increasing separation of knowledge, splitting knowledge itself and then the process of generating knowledge into small entities that increase manageability of specified 'problems' as they emerge from requirements of *action geared to answering immediate needs of daily practice.*

This is to some extent part of the *Methodenstreit* insofar as we are dealing with an epistemological orientation based on positivist-mechanistic understanding of the world, in economics the Austrian School is staring. This is very much a historical approach as it reflects in practice the needs as they emerge from the stage of maturity of the productive forces. We may say – and this expresses a very fundamental issue – it had been research on demand without that anybody explicitly asked for anything to be researched. It is the demand of a hegemonic pattern that implicitly determines the ontological and epistemological assumptions especially of utilitarian individualism.

Research and Education between Politics and Commodity

In this light, a statement as that in Collini's review of *Higher Education: Students at the Heart of the System [Department of Business, Innovation and Skills]* is of course highly problematic. The misleading statement reads as follows:

> Very broadly speaking, the extension of democratic and egalitarian social attitudes has been accompanied by the growth of a kind of consumerist relativism. The claim that one activity is inherently of greater value or importance than another comes to be pilloried as 'elitism'. Arguments are downgraded to 'opinions': all opinions are equally valuable (or valueless), so the only agreed criterion is what people say they think they want, and the only value with any indefeasible standing is 'value for money' (Collini, 2011)

Later in the text we are however led to the actual issue, reading about the intention 'to ensure that university applicants act as fully informed consumers … is to force all universities to publish a Key Information Set, which will include information about courses and their requirements, much of which is already available, plus statistics about student satisfaction, employment prospects and so on.' (ibid.) Instead of being employed by postmodern arbitrariness, we are actually facing a shift towards an instrumentalist approach, specified by its utilitarian perspective on science. Importantly, both, scientist and science are seen as instrumental, subordinated under mechanisms of particularisation.

Looking back at what had been said at the end of the previous section: the orientation on totality on the one side and increasing segmentation on the other side, is not least a matter of the personal dimension: surely in terms of the personal commitment of the individual academic, but more in general the degree to which social relations are relations based on human-based relationality versus emerging from institutional-impersonal relations.

Rather than exploring this connection in its own terms – we may only remind the reader of the Nobert Elias' work on the process of civilisation – I want to point on the most important issue, namely the view on the development of the productive forces that are underneath the civilisational perspective. We come finally to the reference to Adam Smith. Looking at his opus magnum – the *Wealth of Nations* – we read in the fifth book on *The Revenue of the Sovereign or Commonwealth,* where Smith is writing on the *Expense of the Institution for the Education of Youth:*

> If the authority to which he is subject resides in the body corporate, the college, or university, of which he himself is a member, and in which the greater part of the other members are, like himself, persons who either are, or ought to be teachers; they are likely to make a common cause, to be all very indulgent to one another, and every man to consent that his neighbour may neglect his duty, provided he himself is allowed to neglect his own. In the university of Oxford, the greater part of the publick professors have, for these many years, given up altogether even the pretence of teaching.
>
> If the authority to which he is subject resides, not so much in the body corporate, of which he is a member, as in some other extraneous persons, in the bishop of the diocese, for example; in the governor of the province; or, perhaps, in some minister of state; it is not, indeed, in this case, very likely that he will be suffered to neglect his duty altogether. All that such superiors, however, can force him to do, is to attend upon his pupils a certain number of hours, that is, to give a certain number of lectures in the week, or in the year. What those lectures shall be, must still depend upon the diligence of the teacher; and that diligence is likely to be proportioned to the motives which he has for exerting it. An extraneous jurisdiction of this kind, besides, is liable to be exercised both ignorantly and capriciously. In its nature, it is arbitrary and discretionary, and the persons who exercise it, neither attending upon the lectures of the teacher themselves, nor perhaps understanding the sciences which it is his business to teach, are seldom capable of exercising it with judgment. From the insolence of office too they are frequently indifferent how they exercise it, and are very apt to censure or deprive him of his office wantonly, and without any just cause. The person subject to such jurisdiction is necessarily degraded by it, and, instead of being one of the most respectable, is rendered one of the meanest and most contemptible persons in the society. It is by powerful protection only, that he can effectually guard himself against the bad usage to which he is at all times exposed; and this protection he is most likely to gain, not by ability or diligence in his profession, but by obsequiousness to the will of his superiors, and by being ready, at all times, to sacrifice to that will the rights, the interest, and the honour of the body corporate, of which he is a member. (Smith, 1775: 761 f.)

From here it is easy to develop a critical view on the obstacles that are inherent to scientific work as consequence of a lack of a truly social commitment. Already Smith criticises such development of science towards a highly specialised activity, disconnected from complex realities. In other words we find the establishment of self-referential systems: highly specialised but also highly professionalised which means not least highly self-referential. Mechanisms of control are highly protectionist. Professionalisation studies make clear that the orientation on securing quality standards is one side of a coin whereas the other side is the quest for closure, suggesting that only such self-control is real quality control.

ACADEMIA BETWEEN CLOSED AND OPEN SPACES

We may see an epistemological tension along two lines, namely between (i) personal commitment on the one hand and distancing into an apparent detachment, claiming objectivity, on the other hand (ii). This can also be expressed as tension between answering immediate needs and allowing the development of spaces that are open for the future.

		CREATION OF OPEN SPACES – FOSTERING POSSIBILITIES AND OPPORTUNITIES					
		Planned Development of Productive Forces		'Reflexive Responsibility'			
	'General Interest' Knowledge, Formally Reflecting a Given Hegemony				Based on Explicit Social Interest		
DISTANCING INTO 'MATERIALISED' AND INSTITUTIONALISED						**PERSONALLY INVOLVED COMMITMENT**	
Passive Orientation, More by Way of Administering Existing Knowledge						*Orientation on Actively Influencing the Development of Productive Forces as Social Forces*	
	Orientation on Actively Influencing the Development of Productive Forces				*Developmental Productive Forces (Adaptation)*		
		IMMEDIACY OF NEEDS EMERGING FROM THE IMMEDIATE REFERENCE OF ACTION					

SCIENCE/KNOWLEDGE AND REALITY
Science/Knowledge and Steering
Science/Knowledge and Productive Forces

Matrix 1. Science, Knowledge and Reference to Practice.

This can be clearly shown by looking at ac-countability. It begins by establishing a complex relationship that deals with the attribution of investigative processes by way of localising them with reference to certain interests, their social status. As such it includes that the social interest is related to existing practices.

However, as soon as this fundamental localisation is completed, the process can be reduced on countability – 'figures' and rules of arithmetic thinking taking over.

In the words of Sally Engle Merry 'Numbers are the epitome of the modern fact because they seem to be simple descriptors of phenomena and to resist the biases of conjecture and theory since they are subject to the invariable rules of mathematics. Numbers have become the bedrock of systematic knowledge because they seem free of interpretation, as neutral and descriptive. They are presented as objective, with an interpretive narrative attached to them by which they are given meaning.' (Merry, 2008 [July 17th]; quoted in Rosga/Satterthwaite, 2008: 52)

One may see this as loss of totality, disjoining from complex socio-historical contexts or one may see this as established totality – science refraining from working towards its own visionary elevation (meant in a positive sense) or the established knowledge that gains at least temporary hegemony. This is also a temporary 'right' to claim totality of its meaning.

> There is in fact a moment when the impulse to live – since the formal impulse is not yet contradicting it – operates as Nature and as necessity, when sensuousness is an authority, since Man has not yet begun; for in Man himself there can be no authority other than the will. But in the state of reflection to which Man is now to pass over, precisely the opposite is the case – Reason is to be an authority, and a logical or moral necessity is to take the place of the physical. That authority of sensation must therefore be destroyed, before the law that governs it can be established. So it is not enough for something to begin which did not previously exist; something must first cease which previously did exist. (Schiller, 1794: 97 f.)

But this totality changes, becomes totalitarian in character. Schiller, grounded in the ideological construct of *Sturm und Drang,* sees this as positive vision, one may say as realisation of the absolute idea in the here and now:

> Contemplation (reflection) is Man's first free relation to the universe which surrounds him. If desire directly apprehends its object, contemplation thrusts its object into the distance, thereby turning it into its true and inalienable possession and thus securing it from passion. The necessity of Nature which governed him with undivided power in the condition of mere sensation, abandons him when reflection begins; an instantaneous calm ensures in the senses; time itself, the eternally moving, stands still while the dispersed rays of consciousness are gathered together, and form, an image of the infinite, is reflected upon the transient foundation. As soon as it becomes light inside Man, there is also no longer any night outside him; as soon as it is calm within him, the storm in the universe is also lulled, and the contending forces of Nature find rest between abiding boundaries. (ibid.: 120)

However, one may also see it as a temporary success, likely to be succeeded by the fall of the empire which is governed from the cloud-castle. The temporary success had been outlined by economists as Mills, Smith and Bentham, claiming utilitarian laws as eternal and absolute terms of reference. The building blocks can be outlined by five moments:

- it is the individual that takes solemnly his/her decision(s) – without interference from 'external forces';
- as such s/he is solely striving for his/her 'greatest happiness' – something of which even the definition can remain open, being up to the decision maker and in this way underlining the entirely individual character of the entire process;
- however, as much as we are dealing with individual decision-making, this does not mean that it is a simple 'voluntarist and subjective matter' – rather decision-making is based on rational grounds, i.e., it is a rational decision, taken by each individual;
- as such rational decision it refers to 'complete information', i.e., the individual – as individual – is 'empowered' by availability of full information;
- and finally he/she refers only to the rational use of the information, rejecting the possible meaning of any factors that are outside such system of calculability. (Herrmann, 2012: 36)

Having said this, the success was temporary and it has to be further qualified: such success was always socially limited. To the extent to which utilitarianism was able to gain hegemonic power, it was always limited: it worked only as guideline for a small number of privileged groups. And for them it worked only to the extent to which they could actually rely for instance on personal information surplus etc.[1] One can say that it is a matter of the systematic limitation of the homo oeconomicus on a small group of actors, namely those who have the power. Paradoxically it had been the limitation on those strata who did have the pure power of defining the small print of the contracts they concluded with anybody else. – Nevertheless, temporary success means also that the meaning of utilitarianism could only gain real ground – as determination of the lifeworld's ideology – over time, after loosing its immediate role in shaping economic thinking. It plays a more important and sweeping role as methodological individualism in both, everyday's life and in social science. It merges with the one element of modernisation, consolidating the individual – celebrated as gaining independence and availing of the possibility of gaining rights as artificial mechanism for re-establishing the social by a formal structure, with this gaining in retrospect some power.

> Positive law assumes an ordered social context that exhibits certain deficiencies: it envisages more desirable – an ideal – ordering of the context; it prescribes the steps to be taken in order to move the actual towards the ideal; and it orders that these measures be instituted. That is, positive law is at once expository, normative prescriptive, advisory, and imperative. But it is positive law as a means to an end … (Jenkins, 1980: 75)

In short: it is about means to an end without allowing the end to be discussed. Of course, this formulation can easily be misunderstood: at first glance it may suggest the celebration of the previous strangulation of human beings by the corporative state and its inescapable – and uncontrollable – structures. However, reading it in another way, it highlights on the analytical level the twofold alienation: It is the alienation from the 'original social state' as distancing

[1] Thus actually disobeying one of the claimed foundational principles.

the individual from socio-ecological embeddedness; and it is about the separation of knowledge from the process of immediate production – production understood in the wide sense of a relationality: producing 'goods' as matter of producing the conditions and ways of producing social relationships. Thus we arrive at another point of reflexivity: science being prone to external demand emerges from the lack of sociability of the academic system itself: the reduction of communication on formalities.

Outlook – Suicide or Emerging Powers to Self-Recovery

In earlier phases of academic development, the term 'scientific community' had been widely used – and we should not forget that it entailed very much the mutual observation and control: the community as semi-natural peer-system. Though it appears in hindsight and at first sight as world of mutual understanding and support, and is easily glorified by the perception of a discourse within an open group – open for new members and open for new ideas – it had been surely a very closed and elitist mechanism with strictly controlled borders of entry and also strict rules for maintaining membership, individuals paying for defiance with their exclusion. This system, however, has undergone a two-layered suicide (see in this context: Holmquist/Sundin, 2010). On the one hand it maintained its own rules: inward orientation by encapsulation into an ivory tower, cutting itself off from complex soc(iet)al practices by increasing specialisation and finally the dependence of participating in the discourse on membership in the community. This had been briefly broken up especially by the students' and workers' movement in the first decade of the second half of the last century. However, the initial process of a real opening lost momentum by the 'long march through the institutions' (Dutschke), allowing the emergence of the second suicidal layer: 'community members' first adapted to the rules, seeing this as means to an end: the change of the system from within. In actual fact this marks one of the difficulties assessing the situation: undemocratic structures, lack of accountability had been questioned and the bureaucratic apparatus offered an alternative. As outlined already by Max Weber, this iron cage offered an answer:

> (1) The tendency to 'levelling' in the interest of the broadest possible basis of recruitment in terms of technical competence.
> (2) The tendency to plutocracy growing out of the interest in the greatest technical training …
> (3) The dominance of a spirit of formalistic impersonality: 'Sine ira et studio,' without hatred or passion, and hence without affection or enthusiasm. The dominant norms are concepts of straightforward duty without regard to personal considerations. (Weber, 1922: 225)

However, the subsequent problem is that it does not provide a foundation for a substantially 'neutral' power. Instead, we see the emergence of a formal structure which serves privatised interests of a bureaucratic structure of a state which is in a clandestine way privatised. George Katrougalos, Professor for Public Law at the University of Thrate, highlights this, saying (passim, interview in the film Catastroïka)

> Privatisation does not concern only the cases when whole services are taken away from the state, in form of, let's say, concessions. It is also privatisation when universities are evaluated not for the level of education they provide but according to how attractive this education is for the market.

Exactly at this point demand comes into play: everyday's self-strangulation of researchers who give responsibility away by denying that research (as well as teaching) has to define the demand by linking it to human rights. Hans Heinz Holz importantly highlighted that the question is not 'if one is in general agreement that it is not ideas determining history, ..., but the economic conditions' – important is 'if one is ready to accept practical consequences in the sense of equality and justice' (passim).

In this light the problem of research on demand does not only and perhaps not even primarily deal with the question of 'external demand' – any academic work, be it teaching or research, that overcomes the artificial separation of theory and practice defines as part of its own complex soci(et)al practice the existing societal demand and at the very same time it provides an answer.

REFERENCES

Bloch, Ernst (1959): Prinzip Hoffnung; Frankfurt/M: Suhrkamp [written in 1938-1947; reviewed 1953 and 1959]

Collini, Stefan, 2011: From Robbins to McKinsey; in: London Review of Books; Vol. 33 No. 16 · 25 August 2011: 9-14; http://www.lrb.co.uk/v33/n16/stefan-collini/from-robbins-to-mckinsey - 28/09/2011 8:35 a.m.

Greenhalgh, Trisha, 2015: We must do more to tell the full story if impact; in: The Times Higher Education; October 1st, 2015; https://www.timeshighereducation.com/opinion/we-must-do-more-to-tell-the-full-story-of-impact; 04/10/15.

Herrmann, Peter (2010) Human Rights, Health and Social Quality – Realisations and Realities; in: Laurinkari, Juhani (Ed.) *Health, Wellness and Social Policy*. Essays in honour of Guy Bäckman; Bremen.

Herrmann, Peter, 2012: Rights – Developing Ownership by Linking Control over Space and Time; Bremen/Oxford: EHV Academicpress, 2012.

Holmquist, Carin and Sundin, Elisabeth(2010): The suicide of the social sciences: causes and effects; Innovation: *The European Journal of Social Science Research*, 23: 1, 13-23.

Jenkins, Iredell: Social Order and the Limits of Law. A Theoretical Essay; Princeton: Princeton University Press 1980.

Rosga, AnnJanette and Satterthwaite, Margaret L., 2008: The Trust in Indicators: Measuring Human Rights; New York University Public Law and Legal Theory Working Papers. Paper 91. http://lsr.nellco.org/nyu_plltwp/91: 52).

Sally Engle Merry, 2008 [July 17th]: Measuring the World: Indicators, Human Rights, and Global Governance [unpublished manuscript, on file with authors]

Schiller, Friedrich, 1794: On the Aesthetic Education of Man In a Series of Letters. Translated and with an Introduction by Reinald Snell; New York: Frederick Ungar Publishing, 1965.

Smith, Adam, 1775: An Inquiry into the Nature and Causes of the Wealth of Nations. Vol 2; Ed. by R.H. Campbell/A.S. Skinner. Textual Editor W.B. Todd; Indianapolis: Liberty fund, 1981 [photographic reproduction of the edition published by Oxford University Press 1976 – The Glasgow Edition of the Works and Correspondence of Adam Smith].

Weber, Max, 1922: *Economy and Society*; Edited by Guenther Roth/Claus Wittich; Berkley et altera: University of California Press, 1968/1978.

Part I, Scene II: In Front Of The City-Gate

Wagner:
You see a dog, there's no spectre near!
He barks uncertainly, lies down and crawls, Wags his tail.
Dogs' habits, after all.
(57)

Chapter 2

European Policies of Social Inclusion – Fatality of Good-Will[1]

Introduction

European integration had been criticised since a long time for being 'socially blind', subordinating social interests under economic calculi. There are good reasons for taking such view. As commonly accepted, the original Treaties did not offer much in terms of social policy. The European Social Funds and equal opportunity legislation had been the two areas which may be seen as exception – but even there we find the vision of the single market standing implicitly already in the centre of the thinking of the founding fathers. One may even put it metaphorically – their had been only founding *fathers* standing at the beginning of the institutionalised European institutions, presumably being honest in their ambitions of establishing a bulwark against war, but still standing on the harsh foundation made from coal and steel.[2] Only the first elected European Parliament allowed a woman taking a central position on the EUropean stage: Simon Veil, up to then minister for Health in France, and as survivor from Auschwitz-Birkenau surely coined by her opposition against fascism. Thus we may see her in some way as founding mother of a process of European integration that aimed on closely linking the economic, political and social dimension: a position coined by the knowledge of the needs of a healthy body and by the experience of what putrefaction of society means. – Sure, all attempts to capture complex issues like these in a nutshell, are in some way problematic. One point is that social policy already emerged relatively early – in particular the European summit in Paris in 1972 had been a milestone in the context of developing a wider understanding of European integration, seriously considering the importance of living conditions of European citizens. Nevertheless, four points should be clear – and they will guide the remainder of this article: *first,* the European Social System[3] was always founded in a very specific European Economic System. *Second,* rather than being subordinate to the economic interests, 'social policies' had been adjunct and as such inherent

---

[1] The present research had been not least undertaken during the stay at the Corvinus University, generously supported by Balassi Intézet.

[2] It had been the European Coal and Steel Community (ECSC) that stood at the beginning.

[3] I prefer to speak of a European Social System instead of a European Social Model as we are dealing with a reality that developed out of a very specific political-economic context – it is not based, and has never been based, on any blueprint which would qualify it as model.

part of an broader hegemonic system: a late stage of the capitalist mode of production that depended very much on the exceptional path of economic growth, being disposable as soon as this actual growth path would be disrupted. *Third,* the formative feature of European integration had been the idea of a single market, the emphasis laid on the market as a dominant social relationship of 'free individuals' – thus indeed continuing the tradition of the Western enlightenment, founding the idea of the free individual, behaving rationally and pondering utilitarian principles that would guide him/her when concluding contracts. Indeed, the idea of contractualism would guide from thereon the thinking of relationships between individuals and state-building as the utmost incarnation of a paradigms of societies coined by methodological individualism. In an extremely outspoken way the latter had been stated by the European Commission in a letter from September 2012, addressed to Gabriella Zanzanaini:

> As you now, privatisation of public companies contributes to the reduction of public debt, as well as to the reduction of subsidies, other transfers or state guarantees to state-owned enterprises. It also has the potential of increasing the efficiency of companies and, by extension, the competitiveness of the economy as a whole, while attracting foreign direct investment. (Giudige, 2012)

Thus the Social System and its specific characteristics are always coined by the very concrete mode of production. *Fourth,* this is also the core behind the contradictions that are inherent part of the Social System: although it always contains some elements that are genuinely pushing against the border of the dominant mechanisms of generating value (understood as exchange value), there is a systemic mechanism that restricts capitalist social policy on some form of poverty relief. The paradox, however, is that the system tends to fail completely in those times when poverty relief is needed most. Still, at the end we will arrive at the conclusion that we should not really speak of retrenchment. Instead we are more confronted with a period of adapting social policy to the changes of the mode of capitalist production and this means a reshuffling of the overall structures and responsibilities.

WELFARE STATE OR SOCIAL SYSTEM

It is convention to talk about the welfare state – and in particular the Anglo-American tradition subsumes a wide range of different Social Systems under the term welfare state. The term Social System itself needs some qualification in the present context. It aims on replacing both, the term welfare state and social policy (system) – or if not replacing so at least opening a space for thorough reconsideration. The reasoning behind such proposed terminological shift is on the one hand the need to understand 'welfare issues' in a wider sense; at this moment a general reference to the social quality discussion has to be sufficient *(see van der Maesen/Walker (eds.), 1997).* On the other hand it is about capturing the variety of welfare states.[4] This later point, however, needs some further explanation – as it is persistently ignored in the debate *(cf. in the following Herrmann, 2012; Wedderburn, 1965; Veith-Wilson,*

[4] Only vaguely linked to the original debate on Varieties of Capitalism, as outlined for instance in *Soskice, 1999; Soskice, 2000; Hall/Soskice (eds.), 2001*

2000). Only a brief presentation will follow, providing a sketch along the following major lines:

(i) general pattern of generating value,
(ii) resource reference,
(iii) patterns of growth,
(iv) socio-political system and sovereignty.

A brief general characterisation is useful.[5]

Generating Values

In the present context value is initially understood in a rather limited way as economic category. However, this does not mean that we are only looking at the narrow issue of a value-price relationship in exchange processes. At the core of the present interest stands the general pattern of *generating* value. This is closely linked with two issues: *first* the development of the means of production and *second* the move from simple to extended reproduction of capital. It goes without saying that this is not seen as mechanical relation *(see e.g., Eichhorn I, et altera, 1975).*

	focus of the productive process: manufacturing, productive consumption, distribution, exchange	consumerism[6]
rationalisation/ technicisation		
Demand-supply-side economics		

Matrix 2. Value Generation.

There are several analytical dimensions to this: (a) we have to look at the different elements of the productive process, i.e., the *actual production, consumption, distribution and*

[5] Mind that the following is more about providing a very rough sketch, not an exhaustive picture.
[6] Degree to which the economic process is focussed on extended reproduction

exchange as outlined by Karl Marx in the Grundrisse *(Marx, 1857);* (b) to the extent to which generating value is getting distant from the genuine productive process and even developing some independence (the process of disembedding), we are facing a massive shift towards the extension of reproduction: a growth policy that actually looses – in tendency – its link with the production of use value, depending now either on increasing fetishisation of commodities (as visible in branding as major force of consumption) or on increasing artificialisation (particularly relevant by way of financialisation). (c) These two mechanisms are qualitatively characterised by the development of the means of production – at present the special interest is geared to the development of the workforce. It is a function of advancing the *technical means of production* in conjunction with the *pattern of circulation* emerging from the *accumulation strategy* as economic relationality resulting from a *political decision* based in national and global power relations. (d) Later it will be getting clear that this is actually closely linked to a specific aspect of demand-supply relations.

Resource Reference

Understanding political economy as complex relationality means that we are dealing with the definition of borders as lines of reference. The contradictoriness of this definitional process is – at least today – not mainly expressed in wars and international conflicts. More important is the structural paradox that had been highlighted by Philip E. Steinberg, namely that 'the territorial state emerged concurrent with the deterritorialization of political economy and geographical imagination' (Steinberg, 2009: 468).

On another occasion I linked this to the process of structuring the centre-periphery relationship in the light of attributing positions along the dimensions of the overall productive process *(cf. Herrmann, 2010).* Part of this distribution is a matter of relations of accumulation that are specifically shaped according to these power relations. Reference can be made to Samir Amin who – with reference to his own earlier work from 1957 – draws attention to the following distinction:

> Whereas in the model of autocentric accumulation external relations are subject to the logic and imperatives of internal accumulation, in the model of extraverted development, it is, on the contrary, external relations that determine almost entirely the rate and character of internal accumulation. (Amin, 1990: 228)

Importantly, the orientation on a specific accumulation strategy is also determining the 'welfare strategy' of nation states – or we may even say: the latter is part of the first. Going another step further, we can take accumulation as point of reference, recognising it also as fundamentally important matter of defining the relation between use value and exchange value. Although the latter are of course to a large extent matters of commodity production, they are also – and to the same extent – a matter of positioning national production in the global framework of processes of generating different kinds of value. A useful categorisation can be taken from Manuel Castells who, according to Wolfgang-Fritz Haug, presents – for high-tech-capitalism – a hierarchy of four sectors, namely 'high-value production founded in informational labour; high-volume production based in low-cost labour; production of raw material founded in natural resources; 'redundant producers, reduced on devalued labour'.' (Haug, 2012: 156; with reference to Castells, 1997: 146 f.)

In political terms one could even say that we are looking at the foundation for a growth strategy in terms of a reference to different 'raw materials' that specify the various systems, in particular the national economies. In this perspective we arrive as well at a more thorough understanding of low wage labour and precarity. The following matrix can be useful for a tentative assessment.

	high-value production founded in informational labour	high-volume production based in low-cost labour
redundant producers, reduced on devalued labour		
production of raw material founded in natural resources		

Matrix 3. Resource Reference.

Patterns of Growth

With this we get as well a specific take on capital: considering that capital is not just an amount of money but a social relationship, depending on inequality and its permanent reproduction, growth is inherent goal and tendency. As such, it is characterised by the two dimensions which had been already mentioned earlier, namely the distinction between relations of accumulation, the one being auto-centric and the other being extraverted development. For the present purpose mentioning these two patterns is sufficient. However, we have to go as well a step further, aiming on a more sophisticated understanding. Although capital is in principle guided by the orientation on maintaining its character as *capital,* it may differ in terms of its *strategic orientation.* We may call the one strategy *relative economic sustainability,* the other strategy *competiveness.* In other words, we are dealing to a large extent with different strategies of innovation, all aiming on growth. I propose following dimensions for further discussion:

- radical generic versus incremental specific innovation
- endogenous versus imported innovation
- product versus process innovation
- product innovation versus innovation of conditions of production.

The following matrix allows classifying tentatively the different systems in respect of growth patterns.

	autocentric development	extraverted development
relative economic sustainability		
competitiveness		

Matrix 4. Patterns of Growth.

Socio-Political System and Sovereignty

The socio-political system and the stage of statehood reflects in different ways these patterns – not mechanically but by way of establishing complex systems of hegemony in the Gramscian understanding. The obvious questions are first about statehood in the narrow sense and also about so-called governance as political issue. However, in this context we can also see another important topic, namely the question of defining sovereignty via finance policy. Michel Aglietta and Thomas Brand are in a recent publication on *« Un New Deal pour l'€urope »* ventilating this issue. In very broad terms we find the analysis of monetary policies as means of political steering of (in)equality. As part of their analysis we read

> Autrement dit, sans une intervention volontariste de la puissance publique, poursuivre selon ne stratégie industrielle de long terme et munie de moyens financiers puissants, les régions riches deviennent de plus en plus riches et les régions pauvres de plus en plus pauvres. (Aglietta/Brand, 2013: 30)

From there the authors highlight that in particular monetary policies were originally at the core of the processes of 'political nation building': Looking at the important role England played in the development of this modern system, we can easily detect the nexus not least in linguistics: establishing national sovereignty meant depending on the sovereign, the term capturing the royal (and with this national power) and also the money. This gets so eminently clear in Adam Smith's words, insisting that '[t]he first duty of the sovereign, therefore, that of defending the society from the violence and injustice of other independent societies, grows gradually more and more expensive, as the society advances in civilization. The military force of the society, which originally cost the sovereign no expense either in time of peace or in time of war, must, in the progress of improvement, first be maintained by him in time of war, and afterwards even in time of peace.' (Smith, 1776: 707)

The German system presents another facet of this development: monetary policies stood very much at the centre of the new social security system. Although indirectly, via establishing a complex system of insurances, we see a vital instrument that allowed steering money-flows which then defined hegemony in a national and external perspective. Although both are a matter of defining social and class relationships, they are different in that the first is especially about socio-economic redistribution, whereas we are in the second case primarily concerned with political control.

	monetary policy i.w.s. as means of social integration	monetary policy i.w.s. as means of securing international sovereignty
competitiveness		
traditionality		

Matrix 5. Socio-Political System and Sovereignty.

We have at this stage four sets that can be used for analysing welfare capitalism in a more specific way, highlighting specificities and differences not in political terms or as matter of institutional differences, but by way of the character of different political-economic modes that are behind the patterns and provisions of 'social policy'. Some of these factors are surely also quantifiable but at least for the initial analysis it is essential to avail of a fundamentally *qualitative* assessment. Detailed institutional analysis is surely also still important – but it will only be meaningful if we consider these wider conditions. The analysis is not concerned with detecting simple supply systems; instead, we are aiming on understanding the social, defined as

> an outcome of the interaction between people (constituted as actors) and their constructed and natural environment. Its subject matter refers to people's interrelated productive and reproductive relationships. In other words, the constitutive interdependency between processes of self-realisation and processes governing the formation of collective identities is a condition for the social and its progress or decline. (van der Maesen/Walker, 2012: 260)

To recapitulate, the four sets are about generating value, the resource reference, patterns of growth and the socio-political system and sovereignty. These are brought together in the following:

	resource reference		
value generation			patterns of growth
	socio-political system and sovereignty		

Matrix 6. Welfare system – analytical tool.

In the following these will be briefly applied to different systems, heuristically starting from the patterns usually seen as the standard systems, however subsequently putting them into a different socio-historical perspective. The discussion of the different Social Systems will only provide a broad overview. And it needs to be emphasised that we are dealing with some kind of ideal types – the reality is more complex and also the national attributions are only providing first clues, being more heuristic tools and not sufficiently reflecting the fact that in the course of historical development two important features influenced the development.

(i) Considering the emergence of specific Social Systems, these are on the one side strongly influenced (a) by the national socio-political economy and (b) by way of path dependencies. On the other side we have to recognise mechanism of diffusion: experiences made during earlier eras but in different places are also feeding into the specific developments, 'distorting the national path'.

(ii) We find – going hand in hand with processes of globalisation, the emergence of regional associations etc. – processes of harmonisation, most obvious of course in developments as the emergence of the EU as institutionalised Europe, a setting with certain claims of new state-building: although the concept of harmonisation is still strongly rejected, the push towards mutual learning, in connection with the objective push- and pull-factors towards unified conditions and unification, is sufficiently strong to allow speaking of harmonisation, despite all qualification going far beyond simple coordination.

Another general remark is necessary. As much as contemporarily dominant economic systems of production are inherently defined by the contradiction between use value and exchange value, any economic consideration is characterised by the contradiction between the immediate production of socio-individual life on the one hand and the societal process of production on the other hand. One may say that this falls initially together but with increasing complexity of both, societal relationalities and the productive systems we find distortions: mechanisms of mediation play in both areas an increasingly important role. Property in terms of control is surely the most decisive. But we have to go further, looking at property of the means of production, the process of production, the products and finally their distribution. These processes defer on the one hand *between* different modes of production, and on the other hand they defer *within* specific modes of production. It is not least this specificity that defines the different Social Systems. Their analysis requires a thorough analysis of the specific combination of the different forms of meditation. Moreover, it is important that, taking such wider view, we have actually a perspective at hand that allows us also the inclusion of non-capitalist notions into the process of assessment. If we then take property – understood beyond its legal meaning – as indicator, we come to the following overview of property.

	capitalist mode of production	non-capitalist mode of production
control of means of production		
control of processes of production		
control of products		
control of the distribution of products		

Matrix 7. Dimensions of Property.

Social Systems – Patterns of the Social and Welfare State

In the following we will look at the different approaches: social and welfare states, or in other terms: social systems as approaches aiming on securing integration and integrity of systems that are structurally characterised on the one hand by contradictions, on the other hand by 'straight' mechanisms of more or less fundamental exclusion.

The Social State or the Bismarckian Pattern

Dominant feature of the social state is the concurrence of building a (new) nation state and the establishment of a new mode of production. With some justification one may say that the really new character had been the close combination of these two factors: The industrial system had been already established earlier in England, where it had been more a 'pilot project'; and in England the nation building could be easily linked to the natural border of an island nation.[7] These two 'challenges', nation building and tightening the new mode of production, meant, of course, that a new social contract had been needed and importantly such new contract had now also been possible. At this stage, securing stability under new conditions was essential as the traditional patterns of 'social integration' did not have a sufficient foundation within the new framework. The other way round: they did not serve sufficiently to maintain a relatively stable supply of a suitably qualified labour force. Part of the challenge has to be seen in the fact that qualification had been increasingly also a matter of 'social skills' for which security had been a crucial factor – security in particular as socio-economic security and also as cohesion, both allowing developing identification with the system. One may say: the need of manageable, reliable workforce, working within the framework of a system of complex labour contracts, did have as its reverse the quest to grant social security defined in similar, i.e., contractual terms but being as such not simply a 'formality', a legal and administrative issue. Importantly we have to see them as matter of accepting a hegemonic rule: rights, obligations, needs, legitimate expectations, patters of consumption etc. pp had been specifically defined as adjustment and correspondence of accumulation regime, mode of regulation, living regime and mode of life. Economic conditions, social conditions and political conditions worked hand in hand and had been somewhat special due to the fact that this new system established for the first time in history a consolidated version of industrial capitalism, being firmly rooted in the techno-economic conditions of

- industrial mass-production
- within a politically consolidating and expanding framework
- and subsequently aiming on establishing production for an internal, i.e., domestic market,
- thus establishing a political-economic system of external and inner colonialisation.

This new setup had been decisively based on a new mode of distribution and redistribution. Instead of being rooted in patterns of traditional family or tribe distribution, the new model had been very much about class distribution – mainly as redistribution within the working class, but also between the working class and the 'pauper', and to a limited extent also as redistribution between the classes. Actually it can be seen as fundamental break of the

[7] Of course, as today's disputes especially on Scotland and Wales show that this leaves the various problems unresolved until today.

entire system that now the 'pauper' did not really exist anymore. The new ideal had been the rule of dependent work as determining everybody and everything.

Still, the entire system maintained nevertheless a strong traditional stream: as not everybody could be literally integrated into the new system, family integration still played a substantial role – most obvious by defining eligibility with reference to wage earning. Non-employed family members had been only secured via the (usually male) breadwinner. 'Individualisation' and relative independence arrived only much later on the agenda.

The Welfare Society or the Wigforss-Hansson Pattern

The Social System of the Wigforss-Hansson-type, from which much later today's Scandinavian welfare state emerged, was the first attempt of a peripheral country to raise as economic power or better: the attempt to be able to maintain a reasonable competitive position. Background was the insufficient resource basis of the Swedish country which had been challenged to serve as breadbasket for Europe: the climate did not allow developing a strong agricultural foundation for producing sufficiently for the satisfaction of national needs and in addition to this, a surplus that would be large enough to import industrial goods. As political entity, Sweden had been strong enough – the various historical struggles probably welding the country more together instead of undermining the process of identity building. However, the strong identity problem arose from the fact that the national economy did not sufficiently satisfy even the basic needs of the population, leading to a major wave of emigration. Nevertheless, we find at the same time – already beginning in the mid-1800s – important marks of industrialisation. This process had been surely full of contradictions: it had been strongly based in natural resources (as iron, timber); in connection with this, we find to a limited extent processes of urbanisation; it had been strong, however not strong enough to allow developing a self-sufficient national economy. We find an increasing independence and emerging wealth later with and after WW I. This goes hand in hand with a strong wave of industrial investment. Even to the extent to which this had been large-scale investment, both, the economic and demographic conditions had been very much linked into the traditional system of the process of nation building at the periphery of an emerging centre *(see for this aspect of centre-periphery structures Herrmann, 2010).*

Investment into the new Social System, rooted in the idea of the *folkhemmet,* i.e., the people's home, had been based on these objective conditions and the attempt to integrate capitalism from below. Those social democrats, which aimed on establishing this system, had been very much determined by two suppositions:

- capitalism is the major if not only means for developing a prosperous nation that allows production on a scale that is large enough to secure the wealth of the nation's people
- this can only be established as 'capitalism from below' – understood as
    - capitalist large scale production
    - investment being linked to the national community
    - though not rejecting foreign investment
    - and establishing a strong mechanism of redistribution.

Control was not concerned with production in strictu sensu, let alone with the ownership of the means of production. Instead, control was established as matter of working conditions and as matter of distribution. Within this framework a dominant feature can be seen in striving for innovation of existing product(ion) lines, thus 'adding some Nordic character' to existing processes of production. The result was a socio-economic pattern of a 'tamed capitalism' with a partial direct translation of national wealth into wealth for the citizens (not of the citizens), i.e., a common wealth in its true meaning. And even the non-translated part had been in some way translated into national wealth by providing an extensive national infrastructure. The following matters should not be underestimated:

- we may speak of a productivist system of public infrastructure, including social provisions;
- the *folkhemmet* had been a mix of the idea of the people's community and a derivation of paternalism (see *Tunander, 2005*)
- the people's community, not least as amalgamation of the traditional community and the politically controlled, ideologised movement, could function as means of permanent control
- a large part of social integration fostered actually traditional forms of family and community support.

An important field, which cannot be extensively presented here, is the important role of cooperatives and NGOs. In short, they originated in 'lived communities', representing very much the social as it is understood by the social quality approach, presented earlier. In this way they were a matter of integration of production and reproduction of daily life. Coming from this tradition, the cooperative idea could be maintained – and if we refer here to the 'Nordic model', we can see the strong position of cooperative enterprises especially in Finland; and this tradition – the especially strong anchorage of NGOs in the life world – is also the moment that importantly determined the later emergence of NGOs as strong promoters of 'life issues' whereas the issue of providing living conditions by way of service delivery did not play a central role. Taking the typology presented by Ralph M. Kramer *(Kramer, 1981: 9),* we can say that – with all qualification – the Scandinavian NGOs was especially strong as vanguards and advocates, a bit less as value guardians, whereas their role as service providers was less pronounced.

The Welfare State of the Beveridge-Type

The conditions leading to the actual welfare state, namely the 'British model', had been rather specific. The four major issues can be seen in

- the post-war situation that challenged both, politics and economics, to define a place for the country on the global and regional scale,
- mass-consumption was a major development, now especially being a matter of durable goods
- an emerging orientation on service industries

- the increasing need for social competition as part of the competition of capitalism and socialism.

Seen in this perspective, we find only now a really strong role of the state in the provision of welfare. Furthermore it is characteristic that we find a twofold shift in economic terms: the one task had been about re-establishing a functioning, sufficiently developed industrial system that would allow establishing a national economy, strong enough to be competitive and at the same time allowing a policy of relative autarky (while going on to use Ireland as hinterland); the second task had been about establishing an economic system that allows the emergence and stabilisation of a service sector – something that is especially for relative small and semi-open economies rather difficult. One has to remember that England aimed on maintaining a somewhat 'insular' position, on the one hand striving for regaining world power, on the other hand however hesitating to opening itself. That a tunnel was necessary, i.e., that there was a spatial separation from the European continent, was a natural condition. That building the tunnel took such a long time and that, after having been agreed and actually built, it faced hostile reactions, is another issue, indicating the lack of openness. This, of course, allowed also establishing a closed social security system: open for all, as long as they would be nationals; and dealing with everything, by linking it into the understanding of healthy people in a healthy national system: the National Health Service.

Familiaristic Residual Social System

Some countries, though located in and being part of the European centre, remained for substantial time without a properly structured welfare system. Actually joining at some stage the institutionalised Europe meant in many of these cases a more or less substantial push also for the social system. This had been surely to some extent direct and explicit consequence of the EU-annexation: the acquis communautaire meant that several changes had been demanded in respect of equal opportunities, income policies, occupational framework conditions, social and health provisions etc. However, more important is that the major shift was about changing conditions of the productive system. A wide range of issues has to be mentioned – from which only two points that are of special interest in the current context will be looked at: many quantum leaps of the development took the form of implants, understood as alien element, implanted into these economies without being appropriate – Marx highlighted in an often quoted statement

> the fact that labour is *external* to the worker, i.e.,, it does not belong to his intrinsic nature; that in his work, therefore, he does not affirm himself but denies himself, does not feel content but unhappy, does not develop freely his physical and mental energy but mortifies his body and ruins his mind. The worker therefore only feels himself outside his work, and in his work feels outside himself. He feels at home when he is not working, and when he is working he does not feel at home. (Marx, 1844: 274)

This alienation had been multiplied as new industries, occasionally mushrooming as it had been characterising Ireland for some time, had been established in a way that going to work there had not just been about leaving home, but more about leaving the country: we have to see it as abrupt *shift from one productive culture to another.* This alienation gained a very specific momentum by the fact that the development of the social, the shape of 'people's interrelated productive and reproductive relationships' took a highly contradictory form. The following five moments deserve to be highlighted:

- to a large extent, the traditional patterns of social support and provision were maintained,
- thus allowing the lack of political willingness to establish a system of social security and social provision appropriately dealing with the new, though alien trends of the productive system;
- this made it also for foreign investors attractive to use these countries for making a 'cheap rest' *(see with respect to Ireland Herrmann, 2014);*
- however, this did not allow maintaining the traditional structures,
- although the slowly emerging public system had not been able and/or willing to accept the new role.

It is difficult if not impossible to attribute this development in a clear way to one single factor: secular developments play a role as we find very specific, in part even local, factors of family structures and the like; we also find specific national patterns as they emerge from the conditions of competition going hand in hand with for instance EU-competition policies. The result is however clear: social systems that are in wide parts underdeveloped as far as their public character is concerned, emerging private security system and an increasing gap, marked inequality and precarity.

The Harmonious Social System

For two reasons the idea of a Harmonious Social System will only be mentioned en passent: the orientation that is currently prevalent in Asian countries and in particular in China. The one reason for not looking deeply into it is very simple: the author's lack of sufficiently deep knowledge – not least in terms of an understanding in the Weberian sense of the underlying patterns of social structure and mentalities.[8] Admitting this can also be understood as critique of many studies that are currently available, suggesting completely contradictory conclusions and reaching from 'nothing old in the east' as we are dealing with only slight variations of global welfare capitalism to 'nothing new in the east', as the old patterns of Confucian ideology pertains. This leads to the second point which touches upon a very fundamental methodological problem. Put into a question we may ask: To which extent is it possible to understand from outside such system even only approximately? Goethe famously said that

[8] A nasty remark may be allowed without stating the name of the colleague who went for 3 weeks to Japan and wrote an expert book on the way in which traditions play a role in the current welfare provision, *based on this experience.*

Let him who fails and to learn and mark
Three thousand years still stay,
Void of experience, in the dark,
And live from day to day[9]
(Goethe, 1814-1819: 74 f.)

And as much as a researcher, coming from outside, can draw upon the advantage of analytical distance, s/he faces the problem of lacking insight into these 3000 years, taking this as metaphor for lived history. In particular today, an era that is characterised by massive changes as they are also characterising Asian countries, it is without such in-depth knowledge extremely difficult to figure out the different layers and their interplay: the development on the three distinct historical layers as outlined by Fernand Braudel: as traditional view on history of a chronological succession; as history of episodes, we may say ordered by establishing groups around a specific topic; and finally the history of individual events *(see Braudel, 1963: 80 ff.).* This is not just about different 'planes' or stages. But it is about different interlocked political-economic 'systems'. We may mention – and now specifically looking at China – the pre-capitalist structures that are still reaching into today's structurations, the early emerging capitalist inputs, the socialist/communist shaping, though themselves characterised by different phases and the current phase, which may be seen as new-century communist restructuration, state capitalism, imperialist phase of a pseudo-communist system or anything else, surely depending on political gusto; and finally we should not forget that hand in hand with all these different phases there is some global-secular development that specifically shapes the national ways.[10]

Looking from the present author's perspective, coined by educational background rooted in the Western 3,000 years of history, the Harmonious Social System can be presented as attempt based on individual responsibility, while understanding the individual being immediate part of a collectivity *(see van der Maesen, 2012).* The understanding of collectivity, the reference to the 'we', and the role of the individual as part of this collective setting, is reaching far beyond the patterns that can be grasped by subsidiarity and methodological individualism. Some comparison is justified with the Nordic *folkhemmet*-idea, though such view is limited as the latter refers to some kind of provision as core of the home, whereas the Asian model starts from the assumption of harmony. When understanding the *folkhemmet* as people's home, the Harmonious System can be seen as peoples' home where harmony and even identity of interests, references, striving, belonging of resources is point of departure. Compared with this, the people's home remains a gathering of individuals: resources are not genuinely produced in community but they are *ex post* pooled and (re-)distributed amongst the 'inhabitants' of the home – people who are actually in some way (potentially) moving in and out – the small difference in spelling may point on what cannot be really distinguished in pronunciation: the peoples' home standing against the people's home. Leaving the more general moments aside, two aspects are of major interest in respect of the economic situation. First, we are dealing with a tensional relationship between small

[9] Original: Wer nicht von dreitausend Jahren // Sich weiß Rechenschaft zu geben, // Bleib im Dunkeln unerfahren, // Mag von Tag zu Tage leben. - West-östlicher Divan - Rendsch Nameh: Buch des Unmuts

[10] All these difficulties can be well be shown by pointing on the variety of interpretations of the Asian and Chinese development and in particular the highly controversial debate on the meaning of Confucian thinking in shaping the 'Asian Model' as mentioned before.

economic entities, some being small enterprises, but many actually being more subsistence-securing activities on the one hand and on the other hand multinational enterprises. The latter are themselves both, genuinely 'national enterprises with global standing' and multinational/foreign enterprises establishing a basis and/or headquarter in Asia. Second, the socio-economic situation of the people – in terms of income, social provisions, social security – is very much caught in this dualism of a kind of subsistence economy and global corporatist structures. A decisive moment in the comparative perspective has to be seen in the fact that we are dealing with a structural and fundamental dualism that is not a complementing and compensating relationship but a competitive structure: the corporative structures try to exploit the lack of legal enforcement, rely on family support structures etc., while these are under severe threat, dissolving under the pressure of the requirements of the corporate system. At this stage it may be left open if this is a gradual or principle difference between 'the East and the West'. On the one hand it has to be acknowledged that the social systems of the OECD-countries are also very much characterised by and relying on traditional structures; on the other hand it is also important to note that we find a contradictory trend in the development: Asian countries and not least China are strongly oriented on establishing a 'modern social security system' whereas we have good reasons to speak of dismantling such system where they exist(ed).[11] So far we can characterise the current situation only as challenge: a tradition of relatively little developed individualism in its isolationist dictum and instead the importance of the collective identity within which, for which and by which individuality unfolds, increasingly being challenged by the utilitarian individualism of the corporatist system. If, to which extent and how long we can speak of a separate social system has to be left open.

The Forgotten Rest – Increasingly Shifting the Old Powers aside

We have to keep in mind that this sketch is not complete. Both, other 'real' systems and also 'imagined' systems, as they are currently scrutinised in different circles, or systems that are established on a small scale, are completely left out of the previous presentation. An example for the first are for instance recently established systems that establish a link between 'modern Western thinking' and indigenous traditions and specific claims. Examples for the latter are not least the various discussions on Commons, Peer Production and Participatory Economy.

In any case, in some respect the different characterisations are complementing other approaches of a differentiated view on capitalist welfare systems *(see e.g., Todd, 1990; Herrmann, 2011)*. In some respect the presentation above aims on correcting classifications of a reductionist understanding of 'welfare capitalism' as they are dominating the mainstream *(mainly presented by Esping-Andersen; e.g., 1989 and 1990)*. These remained perfunctory not only because of neglecting certain issues as necessary contribution to a more profound systemisation, only adding them at a later stage *(see especially the rebukes of the 'Three Worlds' by feminist critiques and also the debate on the missing consideration of the role of civil society)*. Another and here more noteworthy reason for the present critique is the fact that

[11] To be sure, this is not so much a matter of the amount of money spent but of the reshaping of structures and responsibilities.

the supposed reference to different capitalisms is not really made. Instead, we find predominantly a presentation of different institutional settings within one unquestioned and seemingly unquestionable overall capitalist formation with little consideration of the actual variation. In other words, the fact that capitalism itself changed quiet substantially also in terms of the mode of accumulation, i.e., its economic core, gains only little reflection. Very obvious is that the supposed analytical depth of Esping-Andersen's work had been more a matter of providing a credible reply to politico-institutional challenges of the time for a European audience. Right in time and conceivable in wording, it met a political demand – Michel Albert's work *(Albert, 1991),* but also the increasing number of works on the 'developmental welfare state' proof that the quest for a redefinition of the welfare state and social policy actually emerged globally. One specific reason is the structure of capitalism itself which actually suggests that the globalisation of the economy undermines the conditions of the globalisation of the welfare state. Taking the debate on varieties of capitalism and on welfare regimes serious, we have to keep in mind that '[a]ccumulation is in an entirely capitalist environment impossible. Therefore the impulse of the development of capital from the first moment to expand towards non-capitalist strata and countries, the ruin of crafts and peasantry, the proletarisation of the middle classes, colonialism, 'policies of allotment', export of capital. Only by permanent expansion on new domains of products and new countries the existence and development of capitalism is made possible. But the expansion pushes with its global expansionism towards the conflict between capital and the pre-capitalist forms of society.' *(Luxemburg, 1921: 518 f.)*

This allows us to understand some of the difficulties when it comes to the analysis of the current situation of the welfare state – the assessment between retrenchment and restructuration. Anton Hemerijck suggests that 'if we interpret the welfare state more broadly than aggregate social spending, a finer grained qualitative analysis of long-term policy evolution allows us to paint a broad process of profound, yet gradual transformation of European welfare states across at least five closely related policy shifts in macroeconomic policy, wage bargaining, labour market policy, social security, pensions and social services' *(Hemerijk, 2010: 94; with reference to Hemerijk/Schludi, 2000; Boeri, 2005; Brandt et altera, 2005)*

All this underlines that social policy discussions and the analysis of different social and welfare systems – including the tendencies of convergence and divergence – have to be brought back into the framework of political economy. Of course, some of the reasons are obvious: with the establishment of a more closely institutionally integrated Europe we find new conditions and simple demands from the legal side to redefine eligibility criteria – the coincidence of clearly defined national citizenship and employment systems are fading away and in consequence we need a new framework for policy development; this is closely linked with the fact that the up to (historically) recently favourable economic conditions for the welfare systems are both, structurally and also under the conditions of the still lasting 2007 ff.-crisis under major pressure. Furthermore we have to see that various framing conditions are changing: demographic development, life styles, expectations etc. The crisis has to be seen in a wider perspective, requiring to highlight its general character, recognising that 'comme une crise du système économique et également du système anthroponomique, c'est-à-dire du système qui concerne toute la vie humaine en dehors de l'économie, avec ses quatre moments : le parental, le travail, le politique et l'informationnel (la connaissance, la culture).' *(Ivorra, 2013: 39; see also Boccara, 2010)*

Paul Boccara urges heterodox economic thinking – taken in a wide understanding – not only to criticise the current mainstream but to elaborate moves forward by taking the structural dimensions seriously: 'Cependant, la nouveauté si originale de la crise systémique actuelle, en relation avec de véritables révolutions des opérations techniques de production et de circulation, ainsi que les défis de son tournant récent d'aggravation, demanderaient de poser autrement les questions des transformations pout un sortir.' *(Boccara, 2012 : 101, see also importantly 134 ff.).*

Finally, we have to emphasise that – using world systems theory as reference – the differentiation is not about exclusion but about inclusion: the attribution of positions within the one and only system. This urges us to see that we are not simply talking about economic systems – modes of production, modes of accumulation etc. – relating to each other; in fact we are talking about complex global – world – social systems with different and differentiated forms of establishing and maintaining the social in an interdependent modes.

European Inclusion Policies – Their Structural Limits

In this perspective, the approach of the institutionalised Europe towards inclusion seems to be highly questionable. Six questions, addressing the structural dimension, may be posed in order to support this thesis:

1. *How can one expect a continued employment orientation to overcome social exclusion and poverty?* – Though unemployment is surely a major factor behind social exclusion, it is equally true that the return to full employment[12] is blocked.
2. *How can we even understand what changes are needed in respect of the welfare systems, as long as we do not understand the economic conditions that are performing as framework?* – It is not about the lack of financial resources (actually the availability of money cannot be questioned), it is about an economic structure based in finance and speculation standing against a social and welfare system that is based in 'productive employment'. It is about an economic system that is oriented towards increasing productivity which leads to decreasing employment and decreasing mass-purchasing power etc. – thus the structural conditions for sufficient income for social insurance and/or tax-funded provisions being weakened.
3. *Doesn't the development of the means of production push for changing requirements of life for instance in regard of qualification but also with a quest for participation in society?* – And do the standards of strictly employment-oriented systems, not recognising volunteering, still hugely disrespecting 'reproductive work' etc., sufficiently reflect such changes of conditions and requirements and possibilities?
4. *Do we have a sufficient understanding of Social Systems when we limit the analysis on institutional and employment related matters?* Even if we consider contemporary economic systems as continuously based in employment, the fact remains that this is only a shortcut: as much as GDP is not sufficiently assessing economic, let alone societal performance, it is impossible to reduce societal practice on employment and derivates of it.

[12] If full (time) employment ever existed.

5. *To which extent and in which way is globalisation increasingly shifting towards mondialisation, i.e., a socio-economic mode that makes the world systems a reality not as continued centre-periphery structure but as a centre-less or multi-centred entity?* Power – economic and political – is today surely the main factor determining the ongoing – and increasing – inequalities. However, two main points are increasingly of importance: The questioning of the old centres and the emergence of new patterns of global competition; and the increasing limitation of the possibilities to externalise 'social costs', going hand in hand with this the increasing inequality and exclusion within regions and countries, and some forms of catching-up on the side of the previously (and still) poorer regions and countries. Although this is currently not much more than an emerging trend, it is something that will profoundly challenge the systems of social policy. An additional factor is that the forms of exclusion and poverty are also changing, thus signifying another challenge.
6. *Not least, if growth – measured in standard terms as raise of GDP – is becoming increasingly problematic, how can we justify to continuously consider growth in itself as solution of problems of exclusion and poverty?* – We surely have to consider the ongoing demand for essential goods and with this the need of growth in several areas; but even in these cases the purely qualitative perspective, focusing on employment, becomes problematic. As important as it is to claim the right to work, we have to acknowledge as well that it is 'the first clumsy formula … transformed into the droit à l'assistence, the right to public relief … The right to work is, in the bourgeois sense, an absurdity, … . … [B]ehind the right to work stands the power over capital; behind the power over capital , the appropriation of the means of production, their subjection to the associated working class and, therefore, the abolition of wage labour, of capital and of their mutual relations.' *(Marx, 1850: 77 f.)*

OUTLOOK

Developing a perspective is not easy, as the way to re-establishing the social or welfare state in the traditional understanding seems to be closed, not least by two contradictions. The one is the contradiction between public poverty and private wealth; the other is the contradiction between over-accumulation and wide areas of under-consumption (i.e., the lack of resources to buy even essentials for maintaining mere existence). In short, the first is about private appropriation of social products, the second a matter of the tendency of the profit rate to fall and currently reaching in many cases a level that makes investment unattractive in real terms.

We need new forms of defining power and expropriation. A small, factually barely important, but symbolically decisive point had been – already in 2003 – the decision by the European Court of Justice, highlighting the meaning of fundamental rights and assessing them as more important than freedom *(see European Court of Justice, 2003).* Looking at the judgment, two points emerge as particularly important, highlighting the ambiguity of the entire process: on the one hand the role and meaning of the market is qualified. The judges grant the right that 'the competent national authorities were entitled to consider that an outright ban on the demonstration would have constituted unacceptable interference with the fundamental rights of the demonstrators to gather and express peacefully their opinion in public.' *(ibid.., sentence 89, I-5722)*

The second point is entailed in the perspective that is opened by making this reference and the underlying interpretation. The construal of the commonwealth is very much rooted in methodological individualism: it is the right of individuals to express their opinion and to demonstrate, 'citizens [that] were exercising their fundamental rights by manifesting in public an opinion which they considered to be of importance to society' *(ibid.., sentence 86: I-5721)* – not less, but also not more.

This goes hand in hand with the deeper meaning of the principle of the social doctrine laid down by the Catholic Church at the end of the 19th century, namely in the Encyclical of Pope Leo XIII on Capital and Labor, titled Rerum Novarum *(Leo XIII, 1891)* – and it goes far beyond what the official EU-reception suggests as topical at first glance. More important than the usually highlighted principle of subsidiarity is the attribution of roles and positions, and the rights and duties of the 'proletarian and the worker' and the 'wealthy owner and the employer'. We learn about moral obligations and the need to take care of the other – and it can be read as moral respect as well as providence in connection with the labour force. Leaving god out of the game, there is no mention of rights.

Considering that the European Social Model conventionally refers to this tradition as fountain of its thinking, we arrive at the argument that combating poverty and the attempt to overcome exclusion is by and large characterised by a fundamentally individualist understanding of 'the social', namely a relationship of moral orders and rights, a system of mutual understanding, support and charitability. Here it is not proposed to question these values. However, if and how far such value-orientation can carry a society characterised by fundamental contradictions is as much a question as it has to be asked if a policy limited on moral sentiments can be sufficient to guarantee social positions that are defined in a social quality framework of thinking.

And it is an open question how this will develop in the current situation. It is insufficient to bewail policies of retrenchment and austerity – although we surely have to reject any approaches of that kind. We have to move deeper, however, and analyse in which way the structures that are seen as matter of social or welfare state will actually adapt themselves to the orientation that can be seen as fundamental for capitalist states and regional agglomerations: to establish a strong position in world where everybody *(alluding to the Conclusions of the Lisbon Council from 2000 [Lisbon European Council, 2000])* aims on being 'the most competitive and dynamic ... economy in the world' where 'sustainable economic growth' and 'better jobs and greater social cohesion' are surely not at the forefront when it comes to practice of strategic policy development.

References

Aglietta, Michel/Brand, Thomas, 2013: Un New Deal pour l'€urope. Croissance, Euro, Compétitivité : Paris : Odile Jacob.

Albert, Michel, 1991: Capitalisme contre Capitalisme; Paris: Editions due Seuil.

Amin, Samir, 1990: Maldevelopment. Anatomy of a Global Failure; Cape Town et altera: Pampazuka Press, 2011.

Boccara, Paul, 2010: La crise systémique : une crise de civilisation. Ses perspectives pour avancer vers une nouvelle civilisation, note de la Fondation Gabriel Péri.

Boccara, Paul, 2012: Le Capital de Marx, son apport, son dépassement au-delà de l'économie; Paris : Le Temps des Cerises.

Boeri, T. et altera, 2005: Structural Reform without Prejudice; Oxford: Oxford University Press.

Brandt, N. et altera, 2005: Assessing the OECD Jobs Strategy: Past Developments and Reforms; OECD Economics Department Working Paper; Paris: Organisation for Economic Cooperation.

Braudel, Fernand, 1963: Grammaire des Civilisaitons; Paris: Flammarion, 1993.

Castells, Manuel, 1997: The Rise of the Network Society, Volume 1; Malden/Mass.

Eichhorn I, W. et altera, 1975: Die Dialektik vo Produktivkraeften und Produktionsverhaeltnissen; Berlin: Dietz.

Esping-Andersen, Gøsta, 1989: The Three Political Economies of the Welfare State; in: *Canadian Review of Sociology and Anthropology*; 26, 1: 10-36.

Esping-Andersen, Gøsta, 1990: The Tree Worlds of Welfare Capitalism; Princeton University Press.

European Court of Justice, 2003: Judgement of the Court. 12.06.2003 – C112/00: Eugen Schmidberger, Internationale Transporte und Planzüge and Republik Österreich; http://curia.europa.eu/juris/showPdf.jsf?text=&docid=47920&pageIndex=0&doclang=EN&mode=lst&dir=&occ=first&part=1&cid=2772990; 14/01/15.

European Foundation on Social Quality, 1997: Amsterdam Declaration on the Social Quality of Europe; www.socialquality.eu - general information-Declaration - 28/10/2013.

Giudige, Gabriele: letter to Mrs. Zanzanaini – Ref. Ares (2012)1125135 - 26/09/2012; http://corporateeurope.org/sites/default/files/reply_to_mrs_zanzanaini.pdf1_0.pdf - 02/05/2013.

Goethe, Johann Wolfgang von, 1814-1819: *West-Eastern Divan*; London/Toronto: J.M. Dent&Sons Ltd., 1914.

Hall, P.A., Soskice, D. (eds.) (2001): *Varieties of Capitalism,* Oxford, Oxford UP.

Haug, Wolfgang Fritz, 2012: Hightech-Kapitalismis in der Grossen Krise; Hamburg: Argument Verlag.

Hemerijk, A./Schludi, M., 2000: Sequences of Policy Failures and Effective Policy Responses; in: Scharpf, F.W./Schmidt, V. (eds.), 2000: *Welfare and Work in the Open Economy. From Vulnerability to Competitiveness;* Oxford: Oxford University Press.

Hemerijk, Anton, 2010: Social Cohesion, welfare recalibration and the European Union; in: Zupi, M./Estruch Puertas, E. (Eds.), 2010: *Challenges of Social Cohesion in Times of Crisis: Euro-Latin American Dialogue*; Madrid: Editorial Complutense; 71-149.

Herrmann, Peter, 2010: *Globalisation revisited; Society and Economy*; Budapest: Akadémiai Kiadó, 32(2010)/2: 255-275.

Herrmann, Peter, 2011: The Lifespan Perspective in Comparative Social Policy Research: a Critique of Gøsta Esping-Andersen's Model of Three Welfare States and its Implications for European Comparisons in Social Pedagogy; in: Social Pedagogy for the Entire Lifespan, vol. I; eds.: Jacob Kornbeck / Niels Rosendal Jensen; Bremen: Europäische Hochschulschriften, 2011: 29-49.

Herrmann, Peter, 2012: Social State, Welfare State and Then? Where to Move from the Welfare state? A Cooperative State of Sustainable Sociability as Perspective for

Innovation; in: Heiskanen, Johanna/Henry, Hagen/Hytinkoski, Pekka/Köppä, Tapani (eds.): *New Opportunities for Co-operatives: New Opportunities for People*. Proceedings of the 2011 ICA Research Conference, 24-27 August, 2011, Mikkeli, Finland; Helsinki: University of Helsinki. Ruralia Institute, 2012: 295-313; also: http://www.helsinki.fi/ruralia/julkaisut/pdf/Publications27.pdf - 11/11/2013.

Herrmann, Peter, 2014: Social Policy – Distribution or Mode of Production?; Bremen: Europaeischer Hochschulverlag.

Ivorra, Pierre, 2013: Crise de civilisation, crise de 2008-2010 et solutions systémiques; in: Économie&Politique. Revue marxiste d'économie; 708-709, Juillet-Août 2013; 39-39.

Kramer, Ralph M.: Voluntary Agencies in the Welfare State; Berkley u.a.: 1981.

Leo XIII, 1891: Rerum Novarum. Encyclical on Capital and Labor; Vatican: Libreria Editrice Vaticana; http://www.vatican.va/holy_father/leo_xiii/encyclicals/documents/hf_l-xiii_enc_15051891_rerum-novarum_en.html - 19/11/2013.

Lisbon European Council, 2000: Presidency Conclusions, 23 and 24 March 2000; http://www.consilium.europa.eu/uedocs/cms_data/docs/pressdata/en/ec/00100-r1.en0.htm - 11/11/2013.

Luxemburg, Rosa, 1921: Die Akkumulation des Kapitals oder Was die Epigonen aus der Marxschen Theorie gemacht haben. Eine Antikritik; in: Rosa Luxemburg. Gesammelte Werke, Bd. 5: Ökonomische Schriften; Ed.: Institut für Marxismus Leninismus beim ZK der SED; Berlin: Dietz Verlag, 1975: 415-523.

Marx, Karl, 1844: Economic and Philosophical Manuscripts of 1844; in: Karl Marx. Frederick Engels. Collected Works. Volume 3: Marx and Engels: 1843-44; London: Lawrence&Wishart, 1975: 229-346.

Marx, Karl, 1850: The Class Struggles in France. 1848 to 1850; in: Karl Marx. Frederick Engels. *Collected Works*. Volume 10: Marx and Engels 1849-1851; London: Lawrence&Wishart: 45-145.

Marx, Karl, 1857: Economic Manuscripts of 1957-58 (First Version of Capital). Introduction; in: Karl Marx. Frederick Engels. *Collected Works*. Volume 28; London: Lawrence&Wishart, 1986; 17-48.

Smith, Adam, 1776: An Inquiry into the Nature and Causes of the Wealth of Nations, Volume 2; General Editors R.H. Campbell/A.S. Skinner; Textual Editor: W.B. Todd; Indianapolis: Liberty Fund 1981 [Previous edition Oxford: Oxford University Press, 1976; Glasgow Edition of the Works and Correspondence of Adam Smith]

Soskice, D. (1999): Divergent Production Regimes: Coordinated and Uncoordinated Market Economies in the 1980s and 1990s, in: Kitschelt, H. et al. (1999), S.101-134.

Soskice, D. (2000): Macroeconomic Analysis and the Political Economy of Unemployment, in: Iversen, T. et al. (2000), Unions, Employers, and Central Banks, Cambridge, S. 38-74.

Steinberg, P. E., 2009: Sovereignty, Territory, and the Mapping of Mobility: A View from the Outside. *Annals of the Association of American Geographers* 99(3): 467–495.

Todd, E., 1990: L'invention de l'Europe. Paris: Point.

Tunander, Ola: 2005: Swedish Geopolitics: From Rudolf Kjellén to a Swedish 'Dual State', Geopolitics, 10/3: 546-566 - http://dx.doi.org/10.1080/14650040591003552.

van der Maesen, Laurent J.G., 2012: Orientation, strategies and model (or experience) of the City of Hangzhou (Zhejiang province of mainland China) from a comparative perspective (Working paper nr. 9); www.socialquality.eu; there go to working papers - 11/11/2013.

Van der Maesen, Laurent J.G./Walker, Alan (eds.), 2012: Social Quality. *From Theory to Indicators:* Basingstoke: Palgrave Macmillan.

van der Maesen, Laurent J.G./Walker, Alan, 2012: Social Quality and Sustainability; in: Van der Maesen/Walker (eds.), 2012: 250-274.

Veith-Wilson, John, 2000: States of Welfare: A Conceptional Challenge; in: Social Policy and Administration; 34/1; Blackwell: Oxford/Malden: March: 1-25.

Wedderburn, Dorothy, 1965: *Facts and Theories of the Welfare State; in: The Socialist Register;* volume 2; http://socialistregister.com/index.php/srv/article/view/5952/2848 - 27/08/2011 6:59 p.m.

Part I. Scene XXI: Walpurgis Night

Mephistopheles:
Like this, the journey's not so quick.
(228)

Chapter 3

CAPABILITY AND SOCIAL POLICY – THE SEARCH FOR SOCIAL QUALITY

ABSTRACT

The following chapter will sketch a critique of the fundamentals of social policy and suggest that the capability approach (as other contemporary concepts as for instance Quality of Life Studies, Human Development Approach etc.) are addressing important weaknesses of traditional thinking, however remain in a mindset that is fundamentally limited in two ways, namely

- individualism – and its translation into methodological individualism and
- utilitarianism – and its translation into relations as matter of reciprocal and calculable exchanges.

In a second step it will be argued that Social Quality thinking with its focus on the social, underlines the importance of focusing the productive and reproductive relationships in and of everyday's life. A third section will look at the implications for conceptualising social policy. A fourth section will conclude the thoughts by looking at the consequences for policy making.

THE CRUX WITH THE INDIVIDUAL

In thinking about politics and the foundation of the state in the Western world, one of the main references is the work of Montesquieu. This is founded in the crucial role he played in attributing a pronounced role to the individual as ultimate reference within the modern political sphere.

This had been a crucially important 'invention' in anticipation of the liberal economy – centrality of the individual as condition and consequence of the modern, i.e., liberal economy. In actual fact, it is in the light of today's understanding of the economy and liberalism somewhat misleading: liberal economy at the time had been a truly revolutionary project, geared against the suffocating feudal system. The latter had been based on at least two entirely different principles:

- politically, arbitrary rule had been characterising feudalism, justifying and defending the superordination of land- and war-lordism;
- economically, this had been a modified tributary system which, as such, limited the development of economic activities and subsequently of growth.

Growth had been seen for good reasons as essential condition for increasing wealth for at least a majority of the population, if not even (at least in the ideological dress-up) for everybody who had been 'able and willing to work'.

What became known under the slogan of the Wealth of Nations – this also the title under which Adam Smith's seminal book became known and widely circulated[1] – had been very much the representation of a fundamentally new understanding of wealth: the Commonwealth as common wealth, identifying wealth of nations and wealth of its common people. Subsequently the system of patronage – the landlord being responsible for the welfare of the peasants – could finally be overcome. We have to remember that the tributary economy had been the one side of a complex system which had been complemented by clientelism on the other side. Of course, from there it had been a long way to the later welfare state. Moreover, talking about the welfare state, as commonly suggested by the English language, wipes out the fact that this term is the roof for very different types of regimes *(s. Herrmann, 2012; see also the contribution* European Policies of Social Inclusion – Fatality of Good-Will *in this volume).* Cutting a very long and differentiated story short, we can see the social being re-introduced after it had been widely pushed aside. However, in the course of this development it changed substantially. Four moments deserve special emphasis.

First, even if it is a bold simplification to reduce Smith on the invisible hand,[2] it remains true that the role of the state is in his paradigm very limited; furthermore, it is actually only seen as instrumental for enabling the individual, in particular aiming on enhancing his economic potential.

Second, utilitarian thinking had been welded into the new political economic theory. The easiest way of grasping its meaning is to make reference to the closely linked principle of contractualism, dealing with agreements between formally equal partners, based on free will, dealing with mutual obligations and benefits and they are limited on the content of the contract.

Third, methodological individualism – although in strict terms only introduced at a later stage into social science[3] – had been a paradigmatic approach from the outset. This went far beyond what is usually considered under this term: it had been about systematising contractualism as outlined before as ultimate thought of utilitarianism and transferring it into a principle of life and the new understanding of the social.

Fourth, though theoretically developed relatively late, the marginalist theory of value had been underlying this political-economic thinking from the outset. In short, and focusing on the present argument, it can be translated into a statement concerned with 'just distribution'.

---

[1] The correct title reads: Smith, Adam, 1776: An Inquiry into the Nature and Causes of the Wealth of Nations (Campbell, R.H./Skinner, A.S./Todd, W.B. [Eds.]; Indianapolis: Liberty Classics/Oxford: Oxford University Press, 1976)

[2] Actually he emphasises this explicitly only once, namely in the chapter talking about 'Of Restraints upon the Importation from Foreign Countries of Such Goods as can be Produced at Home'

[3] Max Weber can be seen as founder of methodological individualism as explicit approach in social science *(see Weber, 1921: 13);* Joseph Schumpeter, especially in his work on the Concept of Social Value *(Schumpeter, 1909)* had been establishing this concept in a differentiated way for economics.

The fundamental proposition is that over-accumulation of wealth would actually be unlikely, only happening on grounds of a kind of a 'psychological defect'. In this thinking 'normal behaviour' suggests that with reaching a certain degree of supply, any additional unit would not bring any satisfaction, thus reducing incentives towards 'pure accumulation of wealth for its own sake'.

Leaving aside that these assumptions are factually wrong or need at least succinct qualification – an often-discussed indicator is if altruism is falling outside of the remit of utilitarianism – the present interest is concerned with the paradigmatic dimension. We see that – as matter of the development of the social fabric – the social had been systematically redefined, namely reducing it on the contractually definite relationship between individuals. General practice, political design and academic thinking reinforced each other in this orientation, actually resulting in establishing a kind of restriction of thinking or we may even say self-censorship. It has to be emphasised that we are talking about a redefinition, as we can only then understand that we are not talking about rebalancing economic and social aspects but about a changed systematique. The result of the redefinition had been twofold:

On the one hand the social had been *paradigmatically separated* and *qualitatively sidelined.* Subsequently a separate social sphere emerged, claiming rights against the economy which increasingly violated the security and development rights of the working masses in favour of the freedom of economic activity of the few. This can also be translated into the statement that the loss of the social was a victory of a new anti-social class, namely the advocates of neoliberalism who claimed – later in the words of Thatcher – that there is no such thing as society. These anti-social classes actually made the final step: they reduced explicitly the understanding of the social on welfare issues and went a step further by reducing welfare issues on contractual relations. Furthermore, they reduced any kind of social relationships on interactions between individuals. This however had been the final step to undermine the understanding of the social as complex matter of 'productive and reproductive interrelationships of people in everyday life'. In this way, Thatcher's normative statement became true on a descriptive and even analytical level as much as society had been reduced on the aggregate of competing individuals.

On the other hand, to the extent to which we are concerned with a paradigmatic shift in terms of the formation of the entire social fabric, any consideration dealing with soci(et)al issues, was reduced on relationships between individuals. This meant that thinking was concerned with the search for ways of (re-)integrating individuals into a system glued together by work (employment) and family. The paradox had been and still is that social intervention now emerged as instrument used by the anti-social elements of society (as defined in the previous paragraph) to label the others as …. anti-social. This step was possible as those who are today marginalised, lack the educational, moral and of course not least material means of coping with pure individualism *(see Herrmann/Dorrity, 2009).* – All this is not much more than the age-old game of blaming the victims after their usurped disarmament. In fact, it is not much more than basing the social in its reduced meaning on two pillars:

- integration into an employment based 'anthropological *Zeitgeist*' as outlined by Herbert Marcuse *(Marcuse, 1966. Here: CD 2, track 1: 2.45 min).*[4]

[4] * life is presented and perceived as plight and alienation

- support, if it is provided at all, is grounded in moral sentiments[5] and good will.

Rights are now defined in a de-socialised way: rights of individuals, gained from contractual relationships between clearly defined 'social actors', i.e., calculating, rationally and egoistically behaving individuals.

Can we actually understand against this background citizenship in its true, wider sense? And we have to ask even more: Can we still understand human rights in a generic way? This is at present not of main interest, but at least a quick answer may be given: In both instances the answer is *No.* The only instances for such definitions – if aiming on going beyond contractual relationships – are moral criteria and/or 'add-ons'. A clear example is the *Social Charter* of the European Treaties – originally it had been concerned only with the rights of workers, a matter that replicated the development of social security and welfare systems of many Western societies.

This is an admittedly rough outline, but it is sufficient to allow reflecting in depth about the actual foundation of the various approaches that critically deal with the current state of affairs in 'welfare policies'. It is probably broadly accepted that the current system is facing a crisis going beyond the economic dimension. It is also widely accepted that this is not – only – a matter of lacking finances and wrong or overwhelming bureaucratic rules. One of the very fundamental questions is about the appropriateness and sufficiency of the goals of the welfare state. It seems that it has – paradoxically – pushed considerations about human beings, their everyday's life out of sight. On the one hand it is about a hyper-bureaucratic system, structured by rules and not by people's needs. On the other hand it is about provisions that are defined by utilitarian approaches to the understanding of needs. One of the problems is that political economy is in its mainstream always caught in the conflict between over-accumulation and under-consumption *(see in this context importantly Boccara, 2013).*

LOOKING FOR A RELATIONAL PERSPECTIVE[6]

In a nutshell we may conclude that both, intention and half of the orientation of frequently discussed approaches as capability approach, quality of life research and the like are genuinely valid. Making reference to the main approaches in question and inverting them, we can say that today's societies are

* assessing people by (and providing relevant protection based on) the formal employment status – it does not acknowledge, foster or promote a wider understanding of capabilities, allowing people to adapt to societal conditions in their own terms (referring to the *capability approach)*

---

* however, there is a 'better life': the satisfaction of needs and wants as remuneration of labour – though suffering is the irretrievable foundation of happiness
* life is a matter of striving for being – and the substance of life is productivity with and in favour of society
* refined values are separated from ever day's life, from the daily performance. Finding to yourself is left for the time outside of work.

[5] As well known this is the title of the second main work by Adam Smith, published long before the book on the 'Wealth of Nations' *(Smith, 1759)*

[6] see for the following also Gasper/van der Maesen/Truong/Walker, 2013

* they relate well-being to the income of individuals and the purchasing power, but are challenged to relate not only to satisfaction through commodities but also to the availability of non-material and public goods (referring to *well-being approaches)*
* they neglect the need for human development, going beyond the development of consumers, considering the need of developing personalities under whichever conditions (referring to the *human development approach)*
* they are reductionist to the extent to which they allow making reference to mere existence as sufficient framework for defining rights, thus also allowing a race to the bottom (referring to the *human security approach).*

This list is not exhaustive; nor is the comment on the different approaches a complete reflection on their complexity and multitude. However, the summary allows understanding some of the fundamental problems that societies face today. They can be summarised by bringing them into a matrix within the different approaches can be localised according to their focus:

	integration into existing economic patterns	development of alternative strategies of accommodating needs
emergency/extreme exclusion		
post-material needs		

Figure 1. Needs and Provision.

Each of the approaches can be tentatively attributed along the two dimensions: (i) the relation to the existing economic order and (ii) the relation to the kind of needs they address.

First, it has to be clarified that all approaches are fundamentally based on methodological individualism. On the one hand this is simply about making reference to the individual. More sincere is the fact that in consequence life – individually and socially – is reduced on production and exchange of products, in fact leaving productive consumption and distribution out of the equation. We may quote Joseph Schumpeter who contends that 'it is useful to emphasize the individualistic character of the methods of pure theory. Almost every modern writer starts with wants and their satisfaction, and takes utility more or less exclusively as the basis of his analysis.' *(Schumpeter, 1909: 214)*

It is problematic, however, that he establishes an immediate link between taking the individual as sole reference and the determination of individual decisions by utilities. At first sight it suggests a link to consumption – and it is correct in a narrow understanding of consumption as process of satisfying individual needs. However, a more complex understanding of consumption accepts this, but does so only in a specific way that gives consumption a rather different meaning: 'Production, distribution, exchange and consumption thus form a proper syllogism: production represents the general, distribution and exchange the particular, and consumption the individual case which sums up the whole.' *(Marx, 1857 a: 27)*

Looking at the German original,[7] this has to be interpreted as consumption being the joining up of the other elements. Furthermore, consumption is itself a productive process, i.e., the transformation of the consumed good into another product (as it is most obviously seen when looking at the transformation of raw materials).

These aspects remain unconsidered in the Schumpeterian reading, where consumption is the isolated, intimate process of the individual. – Speaking of the consumer society and in the same breath of individualism and hedonism is a marked expression of this.

Second, the dimension of needs deserves special attention in further considerations – bearing in mind the paradigmatic limitations of the Maslow-hierarchy of needs, we still may use it as heuristic reference, allowing to distinguish between the distinct substantial dimensions defining needs *(see the extended discussion about needs in Doyal/Glough, 1991).*

Third, talking about 'accommodating needs' is in today's global capitalism first and foremost referring to the supply-demand chain of commodities (including defining employment as ultimate condition for making a living). However, the wider reference allows different strategies – from street-level economic activities *(see e.g., Dean, 1999)* to bohemian-style subsistence economy of the post-materialist generation *(see e.g., Lembke, 2006).*

Fourth, mentioning emergence and extreme exclusion is on the one hand a concern of fundamental lack of resources; but on the other hand, usually closely linked to such fundamental lack, is the structural exclusion from the dominant socio-economic mechanisms of production and reproduction.[8]

Having stated at the beginning of this section that 'intention and half of the orientation of frequently discussed approaches are genuinely valid' implies that there is something missing. And this missing link is the fundamental definition and positioning of the social which we understand as 'an outcome of the interaction between people (constituted as actors) and their constructed and natural environment. Its subject matter refers to people's interrelated productive and reproductive relationships. In other words, the constitutive interdependency between processes of self-realisation and processes governing the formation of collective identities is a condition for the social and its progress or decline.' *(van der Maesen/Walker, 2012: 260)*

Of course, it would be naïve to deny the simple truth that 'collectivities must be treated as solely the resultants and modes of organization of the particular acts of individual persons, since these alone can be treated as agents in a course of subjectively understandable action.' *(Weber, 1921: 13)*

However, this does by no means justify the complex paradigm that became known as methodological individualism and which had been briefly discussed earlier. The quandary is not the reference to individual action as such; the problem is that in the given way, i.e., due to its intimate link to utilitarianism, it makes it impossible to understand the complexity of *social praxis.*

It finds its most obvious expression in the segregating structure of both, cognition and political practice. The established approach, coined by basing the social in individual utilitarian behaviour, can be presented in the following way:

---

[7] 'Konsumtion die Einzelnheit, worin sich das Ganze zusammenschließt.' *(Marx, 1857: 11)*

[8] As mentioned in the previous point the supply-demand chain of commodities (including the need of employment as ultimate condition for making a living. It may be noted that extreme poverty in many of the so-called developing countries is very much linked to the emerging integration into the global-capitalist system which only held a peripheral role for them.

Utilitarian Orientation as Criteria for Valuation				
Economic Dimension	Social Dimension	Cultural Dimension	Environmental Dimension	… … … …

Figure 2. Utilitarian design of realities.

In some respect we may speak of non-communicating vessels – based on a zero-sum-assumption, and taking the status quo: dominated by neo-liberal economic thinking and practice as unchangeable. The problems are obvious: sub-systemic functionality may be enhanced; however, systemic functionality is diminished or even completely undermined. Furthermore, dysfunctions may be temporarily or partly or regionally overcome by exchange between the pillars. In economic terms this would be about the internalisation of externalities (for instance by making environmental protection profitable; or including people outside of the employment system into employment based social insurance systems). However, the structural faultiness remains in place. The problem – and this is shown by the figure – is that the dominance of the economic dimension is translated into an overarching way of thinking that determines even the non-economic dimensions of the social fabric.

Taking a fundamentally different stance, the expressionist approach starts from focusing on everyday's life and with this it concentrates on 'what people really do'. This is a relational perspective, contending that '[r]elationships are not just the interactions of what was originally nonrelational; relationships are relational 'all the way down.' Things are not first self-contained entities and then interactive. Each thing, including each person, is first and always a nexus of relations.' *(Slife, 2004: 159)*

While this definition may sound abstract, is in actual fact very concrete: it is not the abstract segregated action – economic activities, social activities as matter of interactions between individuals, cultural activities etc. pp. as distinct realms, often competing with each other – but the generic and integrated social activity following the definition of the social quality approach (see above) that stands at the centre, being point of departure and at the very same time result of praxis. The following is an attempt to visualise this relationality as core of the understanding of social praxis.

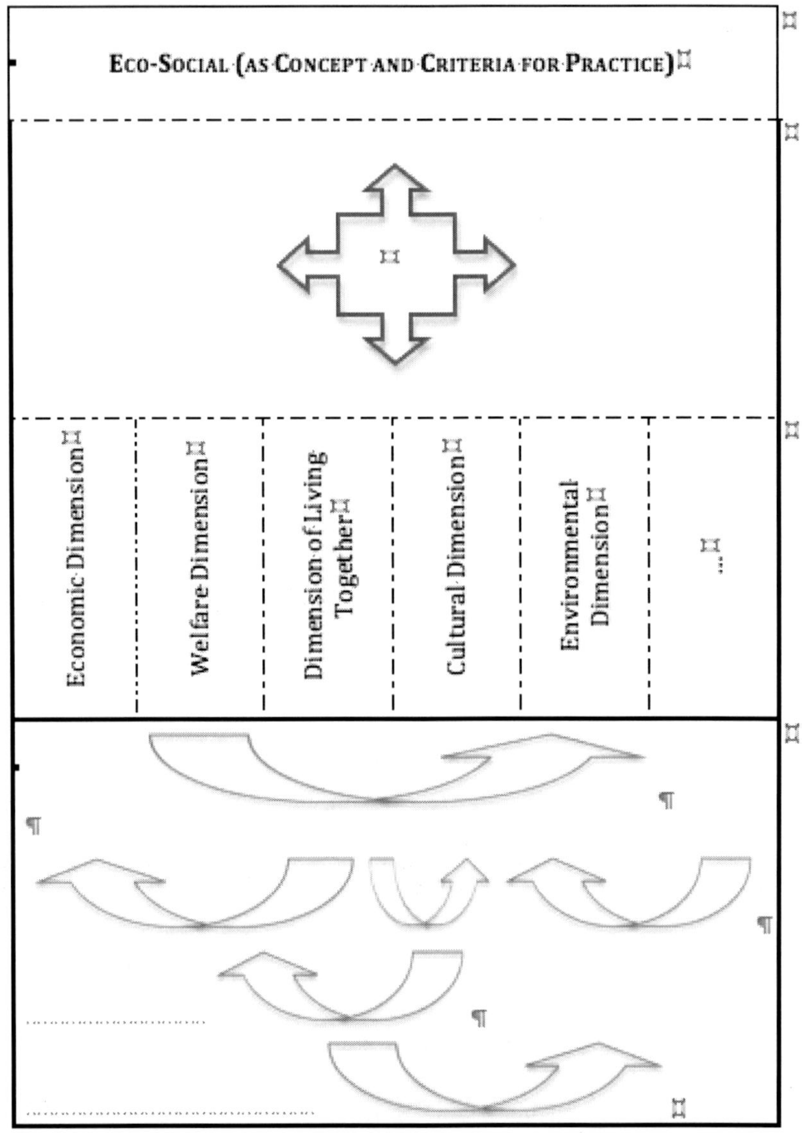

Figure 3. Relational Approach.

Social Policy – A Praxis Perspective

By now it should be clear that the four (exemplary) approaches, namely the capability approach, well-being approaches, the human development approach and the human security approach are hugely important in the search for a new agenda. However, before discussing such new agenda further, we have to present at least the core reasoning behind the need for such renewal.

- We find an aggravation of global inequalities – notwithstanding the notion of a tendency towards a u-turn of development, the up-to-now poor countries catching up, the fact of persisting inequality cannot be denied even if this u-turn can be significantly evidenced.[9] Furthermore, this is not simply an empirically overwhelming 'injustice' but an intersection that questions the systemic functioning.[10]
- The ideological statement, proposing that the raising tide lifts all boats, has been proven in the global perspective and also in the various national perspectives as wrong and at most mere wishful thinking. We may even speak of a reversal: in countries with an extreme boom as Ireland before the crisis we find exactly during the phase of extreme growth increasing inequality and even impoverishment of many people; we saw also major pressure on working and living conditions and a major imbalance in the social care system;[11] on the other hand, if any, those countries with an active re-distributional policies managed also well in developing a more modest, but sustainable economic growth – we may speak of an integrated approach of socio-economic development *(cf. Herrmann/Heshmati/Tausch/Bajalan).*[12]
- Important is also to recognise the increasing pressure on the value systems – both, lack of readiness to solidarity and search for meaning may be highlighted as two issues that actually express a variety of issues, by and large headed by the mismatch of conditional and constitutional factors, translated into a kind of anomie in the realm of normative factors.
- And of course, the material conditions needed for answering these challenges are also under pressure: the 'old welfare systems' – in their historicity – had been shaped by specific patterns of the underlying mode of production within a global context. This is true for instance for the Bismarckian, the Wigforss-Hansson and the Beveridge-model. The way of financing had been adopted from these conditions, and could even be maintained for some time beyond the full feasibility of each of the models. However, we have to see that the economic system entered a new stage *(the change of the regime of capitalist accumulation)* and that we face a developmental stage where capitalism has to be overcome in a more fundamental way *(quest for a new mode of production).*

Taken together, we are confronted with a fundamental challenge in which the crisis of the economic system and the system of socio-humane existence *(système anthroponomique)* are merging into a general crisis *(cf. Boccara, 2010; see also Ivorra, 2013: 39).*

Earlier we had been briefly dealing with the translation of the traditional foundation of social science in contemporary approaches into some fundamental lines of needs and provision of relevant means (see Figure 1). On the one hand such perspective is inclined to restrict the view on agency: in the given perspective we have individuals who fail to secure their means in a sufficient way, standing somewhat against – usually statutory – actors, being

---

[9] See e.g., Malik, 2013

[10] The fact of accumulation of private wealth while public poverty is increasing is surely not new but plays a renewed relevance.

[11] Social care system here understood also in terms of the 'welfare mix'.

[12] It is noteworthy here that the so-called 'flexicurity' policy had been more or less a child born in the propaganda departments of the European headquarters.

as 'last resort' responsible for securing people's existence. To some extent we find a switch tower in the middle: the statutory agency trying to shift responsibility (back) to the individual. The strategic pillar is the principle of subsidiarity. On the other hand this way of thinking has structural problems in considering issues of reproduction and relationships in another way than as matter of 'defence against interests of the realisation of capital'. There are surely good reasons for taking such defensive perspective: finally we are living in a world that is dominated not only by capitalist thinking in general, but more concrete by its neo-liberal variation. Nevertheless, we propose that the tensions proposed in Figure 1 are not grasping the real problematique behind social policy. The Social Quality Approach refers to two main dialectical tensions that provide a major point of reference for both, society building and social policy in the new understanding. These are presented in the following Figure 4.

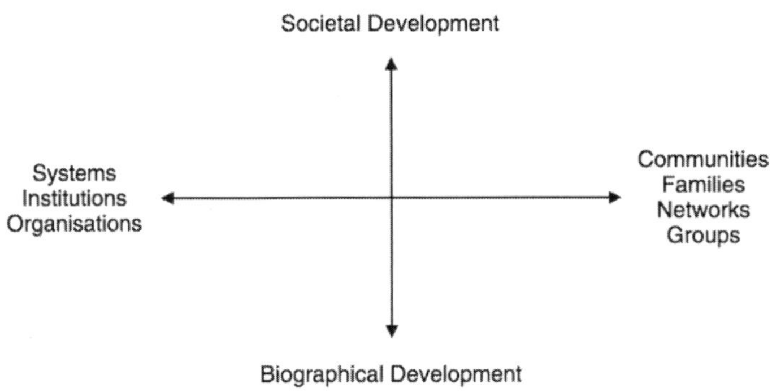

(from: Beck/van der Maesen/Walker, 2012: 51)

Figure 4. Interplay between two basic tensions.

Taking this as focus for conceptualising a new approach to social policy further, we have arrived at new parameters that allow analysing circumstances of life not only by way of looking at 'individuals in context'. Instead, we can now go further and approach both, the analytical level as well as policy making as relational. The fundamental suggestion is the same as that Fabio Folgheraiter claims for social work, contending that it 'is a science of the possible, not, as Husserl says, 'a mere science of the matter of fact'; it is science of the human sense and shared understanding of what is today, or may be tomorrow, a *common good ... .' (Folgheraiter, 2012: 53; with reference to Donati/Solci, 2011; see already Bloch, 1959: 258-288)*

The architecture consists of conditional, constitutional and normative factors. Though it is not entirely correct, we may use a shortcut for the explanation, suggesting conditional factors as matter of the objective situation, the constitutional factors as matter of subjectivity – comprising subjective assessment but importantly also the subject in terms of the genuine actor – and the normative factors as underlying and guiding values. It is important to notice that the link between the three sets of factors is also relational – they cannot be taken as such, but are defined in their mutual reference. This means that we are dealing with reflexive processes that put social policy in a perspective that is different from the mainstream:

It focuses on the needs of people as active citizens, where citizenship is not understood solely as participating in a given societal setting – instead we are now dealing with a more complex view on empowerment. It is not about empowering people to be fully part of the given system; nor is it understood as empowerment by way of developing 'own capacities' that allow being part in terms of functioning in the understanding suggested by Amartya Sen. Instead, we move a step further by suggesting that real empowerment has to be about the co-production of the soci(et)al fabric.

The following theses can summarise the meaning of the social quality theory for developing a new understanding of social policy.

1. Social Policy Is About Provision of Basic Needs

Of course, securing life has to be essential – and presumably this is a consensus that reaches across all considerations that can be seen as matter of social policy in the widest sense. Still, even here is one point that distinguishes the social quality thinking from other approaches: life is not seen as mere existence but taken serious as matter of living, i.e., securing a standard of life that allows explicitly for dignity as matter of socio-individual self-determination. And as such it is part and parcel of the complex socio-natural metabolism.

2. Social Policy Is About Active Involvement

This second point is most likely also a widely shared orientation. The two distinctive moments in a social quality perspective are the following

- Social Quality Thinking is orienting on involvement not in terms of integration in the chain of commodity production and consumption but going beyond, appreciating other forms of production and exchange;
- it is also orienting on including non-marketable activities as core of the approach to social policy – such involvement is not understood as 'end' in terms of being a consequence of other forms but it is meant to be an end in its own right.

There is an additional aspect to it: analysis, when employing social quality thinking, is already intrinsically part of the policy making process, not only by way of participative research and consultation; beyond that, it is also in its iterative understanding a matter of continuously – uno actu – developing praxis through analysis.

3. Social Policy Is About the Environment

The term environment is actually already somewhat problematic as it is in the common understanding an externality.[13] By contrast, the definition of the social highlights the 'interaction between people (constituted as actors) and their constructed and natural environment', and this means carrying the social space as permanent reference, seeing human action as shaped by and shaping the environment. In particular the work on sustainable urban development is hugely important in this respect. It is useful to speak of an eco-social entity,

[13] See in this context cum grano salis the quote from This Saint-Jean, page 8

thus emphasising that urban spaces are in any case socio-ecological systems – this includes that they are shaped by the people living there and it equally includes that the way of life is shaped by these systems. And we are talking about conditions in terms of limitations and opportunities.

This complements the problem of overcoming the 'disembedding' and 'separation' of economy and social. In fact we can apply cum grano salis '[w]hen authors state that 'economic facts' are 'embedded' in the social … they suppose that there is something we can identify as 'economic' which at the same time can be distinguished from the 'social' … In a way, they are themselves drawing the boundary they are trying to question.' *(This Saint-Jean, 2005: 318f., translation P.H.)*

4. Social Policy Is About Finances

Of course, finances – as input for relevant measures but also as output in form of cash-payments, service provision or being transformed into in-kind support – are crucial. And obviously financial sustainability is of utmost importance. A crucial aspect is, however, to look at the issue of finances not only in budgetary terms. Equally important is opening the view on the real costs and contributions. Subsidies are surely one point in question – and stating this is not primarily a question about allowing subsidies or not allowing them; instead, the quality of such spending has to be the relevant parameter, the fundamental issue being

- securing overall quality, for instance of services, including the working conditions of staff
- making externalisation in time and/or space impossible (for instance increasingly an issue when we look at 'health-tourism' *(see e.g., Klar, 2013)*
- it is important to tackle the financing system already at the outset – social justice cannot be reduced on redistribution (alone) after allowing fundamental injustices at the outset
- the last remark includes the need to rethink the value system in economic terms – generating income, based in the idea of commodity exchange in a utilitarian fashion, makes even in mathematical terms only sense if it the definition is limited on grasping increasing profitability.

5. Social Policy Is About Culture

Debates on social policy make frequently reference to the social fabric, highlighting the need to think not only about the structures and institutions that provide a framework within which people live. Especially here is a major challenge. It is more appropriate to speak of hegemonic systems – it had been implicitly shown throughout this text that it is impossible to derive a clear understanding of needs, wants and expectations and also the understanding of rights, provisions and obligations by reference to general values. The only valid definition comes from societal praxis – and this is caught in the need to replicate the hegemony, as long the hegemony is also the source of material resources. Only establishing a counter-hegemony allows opening up fundamentally new options.

6. Social Policy Is About Social Work

Social work is surely something that is not clearly defined, gaining different meanings from national traditions and contexts, each defining allowing a fundamental consensus for accepting and rejecting intervention. A major difference is also the link that is seen and established between social work and social policy. However, there is an increasing debate in social work theory and practice, aiming on establishing the relational character. Fabio Folgheraiter elaborates in this context not least the role played by subjectivity – especially as matter of everybody being subject in the twofold sense. In his words '[w]e need a 'humanistic' theory which can treat positivism from the phenomenological standpoint, and phenomenology from a positivist standpoint. We need an ambivalent – relational(.) – theory which is both positivist and its opposite at the same time.' *(Folgheraiter, 2012: 45)*

Though social work was historically always trapped in the tension of affirmative hegemonic action and emancipative processes, torn between depending on resources of 'the system' and being completely incorporated *(see e.g., Lipsky, 1980)* and committed to the values of liberation, social policy has to answer seriously the challenge of calling for emancipative social work within its own framework, understanding the two as integral sides of the overall system of working for social quality.

7. Social Policy Is About (New Forms Of) Democracy

This necessarily implies striving for new forms of democracy. First, asking for new forms does not mean forgetting the old ones: the parliamentary system – with all necessary critique and also with all possibly complementing forms of direct democracy – is and will be essential for the foreseeable future. Second, there is a need for further elaboration and structural change, allowing dealing with an emerging 'global citizenship'. Third, however, we face the (by no way new) challenge of anchoring democracy in everyday's life.

8. Social Policy Is About Education

Education is one of the most crucial aspects in this respect; however it is not simply a matter of knowledge transfer and development of skills by a 'social investment' strategy. Instead we have to take up the challenge of thoroughly developing an understanding that links into the humanist traditions, while overcoming at the same time the individualist grounding of enlightenment thinking.

9. Social Policy Is About Global Citizenship

Many, if not all problems that are today seen as core challenges of agendas of social interventions, are due to some form of externalisation: living on the back of the future; pushing the costs of 'our welfare' to other regions and countries; allowing 'a better life' of some and accepting the price of huge inequalities; and not least, striving for success in one political arena while accepting emerging costs in other areas. Calling for global citizenship highlights the need of incorporating the external 'costs' as much as possible into any balance sheet, thus not least by looking for a substantial take on costs, i.e., an understanding that looks at the qualitative aspects *(see already above on page 8 the remark on cost).* In such perspective, globalisation surely gains a new understanding, fundamentally different from moving further to global capitalism. Now, global justice and responsibility – principles that are of utmost importance in social quality thinking – gain also a new understanding. They are not grounded in moral values and norms but in a new understanding of political economy. A surely difficult question is that of global respect as it is too often irresponsive when it comes to the question of contradicting systems.

10. Social Policy Is About Developing Local Praxis

This is also an important difference to social-policy-making in the traditional sense – and with this also to the capability approach. We are not talking about simple or complex relationships of exchange.

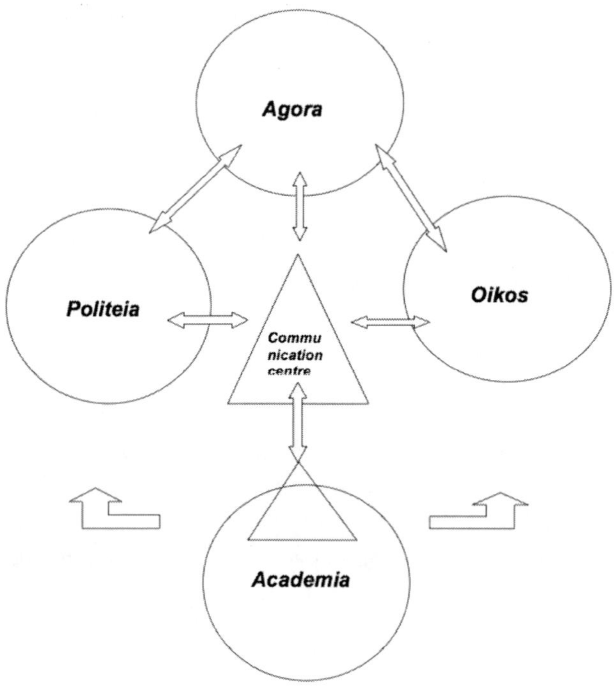

(taken with a minor change from van der Measen, 2012: 11).

Figure 5. Framework for the Strategies of the Dutch city of The Hague.

On the one hand this means that the social or welfare state (or any functional equivalent) is promoting, (re-)distributing, helping, penalising, activating citizens – as any traditional understanding of social policy suggests. On the other hand it is not about the development, promotion and maintenance of individuals' capabilities, enabling them to 'take part in society'.

Reading these formulations carefully should make clear that the two approaches are in actual fact not very dissimilar. We are dealing with a field of contestation and collaboration in which – on different levels and not least locally – the socio-ecological systems are shaped by way of the people interacting among each other and with their environment by way of mutual (re-)production.

The following Figure 5 shows a framework for such discourse which had been developed during the work in Laak, a quarter of The Hague in The Netherlands, applying the social quality approach as guiding developing an urban area.

Summary and Conclusion

The crucially important point is that social quality theory allows sublation and supersession of approaches as the capability approach, well-being approaches, the human development approach or the human security approach in a dialectical way. All of these approaches raise serious concerns and weaknesses of contemporary policies, and highlight important challenges; these are namely

- the need to emphasise capabilities instead of reducing political strategies on integration into the labour market
- the need to go beyond utilitarian thinking which takes GDP as indicator of societal wealth and sees well-being as matter of increasing purchasing power
- the need to look for an enhanced understanding of development, inherently linked to the development of empowered personalities
- the need to understand human security as matter that has to go already at its very basic stage beyond securing mere existence.

However, at the very same time the social quality approach suggests going further. *First,* of special importance is the search for an alternative economic framework that allows integrating production and reproduction of everyday's life. *Second,* furthermore, as everyday's life is according to social quality thinking genuinely a social process, it is necessary to redefine a (human) rights based approach by searching for a fourth generation of human rights, dealing with the mode of production. *Third,* it is also a matter of establishing new relationships between the various actors. However, as issue of 'glocal praxis' it is not simply a matter of finding new structures and institutions. Instead, it is about finding an appropriate way of dealing with the two fundamental tensions that had been outlined in Figure 4. *Forth* and finally – and this is surely the most difficult point – the integration of all these different factors into one coherent approach is essential: All aspects allow only in their mutual complementarities and integration fundamentally new steps. This means in a nutshell that we have to detect the underlying and inherent mechanisms of socialisation that are inherent in the overall process, even if at odds with individualisation that we face at first sight.

REFERENCES

Beck, W., van der Maesen, L. J. G., and Walker, A., 2012. *Theoretical foundations*. In: L. J. G. van der Maesen and A. Walker, eds. Social quality: from theory to indicators. Basingstoke: Palgrave Macmillan: 44–69.

Bloch, Ernst, 1959: Prinzip Hoffnung; Frankfurt/M: Suhrkamp [written in 1938-1947; reviewed 1953 and 1959]: 258-288.

Boccara, Paul, 2010: La crise systémique : une crise de civilisation. Ses perspectives pour avancer vers une nouvelle civilisation, note de la Fondation Gabriel Péri.

Boccara, Paul, 2013: Théories sur les crises. La suraccumulation et la dévalorisation du capital. Sur les fondements des crises du capitalisme, leur nécessité systémique, leurs issues, les transformations et la mise en cause du système. 1mre volume : Analyses fondamentales et des bases des crises cycliques de moyenne période; Paris : éditions delga.

Dean, Hartley, 1999: Begging Questions: Street-level Economic Activity and Social Policy Failure; Bristol: Policy Press.

Donati, P./Solci, R. 2011: I beni relazionali: Che cosa sono e cosa producono; Torino: Bollati Boringhieri.

Doyal, Len/Glough, Ian, 1991: A Theory of Human Need; Houndsmills et altera: Macmillan.

Folgheraiter, Fabio, 2012: The mystery of social work. A critical analysis of the Global Definition and new suggestions according to the Relational theory; Trento: Edizioni Erickson.

Gasper, Des/van der Maesen, Laurent J.G./Truong,Thanh-Dam/Walker, Alan, 2013: Connecting 'Human' and 'Social' Discourses: The Human Development, Human Security and Social Quality Approaches; in: Otto, Hans-Uwe/Ziegler, Holger (eds.): Enhancing Capabilities: The Role of Social Institutions; Opladen/Farmington Hills, MI: Barbara Budrich Publishers: 13–39.

Herrmann Peter/Dorrity, Claire, 2009: Critique of Pure Individualism; in: Dorrity, Claire/Herrmann, Peter [eds.]: Social Professional Activity – The Search for a Minimum Common Denominator in Difference; New York: Nova Science, 2009: 1-27.

Herrmann, Peter, 2012: Social State, Welfare State and Then? Where to Move from the Welfare state? A Cooperative State of Sustainable Sociability as Perspective for Innovation; in: Heiskanen, Johanna/Henry, Hagen/Hytinkoski, Pekka/Köppä, Tapani (eds.): New Opportunities for Co-operatives: New Opportunities for People. Proceedings of the 2011 ICA Research Conference, 24-27 August, 2011, Mikkeli, Finland; Helsinki: University of Helsinki. Ruralia Institute, 2012: 295-313; also: http://www.helsinki.fi/ruralia/julkaisut/pdf/Publications27.pdf

Herrmann, Peter/Heshmati, Almas/Tausch, Arno/Bajalan, Chemen S.J., 2008: Efficiency and Effectiveness of Social Spending; Bonn: Institute for the Study of Labor (IZA); Cologne - [Discussion Paper 3482].

Ivorra, Pierre, 2013: Crise de civilisation, crise de 2008-2010 et solutions systémiques; in: Économie&Politique. *Revue marxiste d'économie*; 708-709, Juillet-Août 2013; 39-39.

Klar, Andreas, 2013: Gesundheitstourismus in Europa. Eine empirische Transaktionskosten-Analyse; Baden-Baden: Nomos.

Lembke, Judith, 2006: Verdrängungskünstler in Berlin; Niedrige Mieten und fehlende Arbeitsplätze fördern die Selbstständigkeit von Kreativen in der Hauptstadt; in: Frankfurter Allgemeine Zeitung; Nr 222; 23.09.2006: 15.

Lipsky, Michael, 1980: Street-level bureaucracy: Dilemmas of the individual in public services; New York: Russell Sage Foundation.

Malik, Khalid [director and lead author); United Nations Development Programme, 2013: Human Development Report 2013. The Rise of the South: Human Progress in a Diverse World. Published for the United Nations Development Programme (UNDP); New York: UNDP

Marcuse, Herbert, 1966: Der Mensch in einer sozialisierten Welt. Aufnahme: 03.10.1966, BR Technik: Schmitt Laufzeit: 47:13; CD 2: track 1: 2.45 min; from: Der Mensch in einer sozialisierten Welt. Originalvorträge von Herbert Marcuse. Autor: Herbert Marcuse. Sprecher: Herbert Marcuse. Aus der Reihe: O-Ton-Wissenschaft. Thema: Soziologie, Wissenschaft. 4 CDs - ca. 200 Minuten: CD 2: track 1: 2.45 min.

Marx, Karl, 1857 (a): Economic Manuscripts of 1957-58 (First Version of Capital). Introduction; in: Karl Marx. Frederick Engels. *Collected Works*. Volume 28; London: Lawrence&Wishart, 1986; 17-48.

Marx, Karl, 1857 (b): Grundrisse der Kritik der Politischen Ökonomie (Rohentwurf). 1857-1858. Anhang 1850-1859; Berlin: Dietz Verlag, 1974.

Schumpeter, Joseph, 1909: On the Concept of Social Value; in: The Quarterly Journal of Economics; Oxford University Press; Vol. 23, No. 2: 213-232; Stable URL: http://www.jstor.org/stable/1882798.

Slife, Brent F., 2004: Taking Practice Seriously: Toward a Relational Ontology; in: *Journal of Theoretical and Philosophical Psychology*; 24.2; 157-178.

Smith, Adam, 1759: The Theory of Moral Sentiments; D.D. Raphael/A.L. Macfie [eds.]; Indianapolis: Liberty Fund, 1976.

This Saint-Jean, Isabelle, 2005: Peut-on définir la sociologie économique?, in: Philippe Steiner and Isabelle This Saint-Jean (eds.): Sociologies Économiques. L'Année sociologique 55 (2005); http://www.cairn.info/revue-l-annee-sociologique-2005-2-page-307.htm - 09/09/2014; DOI: 10.3917/anso.052.0307 http://www.cairn.info/load_pdf.php?ID_ARTICLE=ANSO_052_0307 - 01/01/15: 307 – 326: here: 318f., translation P.H.

van der Maesen, Laurent J.G./Walker, Alan, 2012: Social Quality and Sustainability; in: Van der Maesen, Laurent J.G./Walker, Alan (eds.): Social Quality. From Theory to Indicators: Basingstoke: Palgrave Macmillan; 250-274.

van der Measen, Laurent, 2012: Working-paper nr. 9: elaboration of a lecture on the orientation, strategies and model (or experiences) of the City of Hangzhou (Zhejiang province of mainland China), from a comparative perspective.

Weber, Max, 1921: Economy and Society. An Outline of Interpretive Sociology; Edited by Guenther Roth and Claus Wittich; Berkley et altera: University of California Press; 1978; vol 1.

Scene The Cathedral

The Evil Spirit
Wrath grasps you!
The trumpet sounds!
(225)

http://artmatters.ca/wp/wp-content/uploads/2010/06/faust2.jpg - 04/01/15

Chapter 4

SOCIAL QUALITY – SOCIAL ANOMIE. TWO SIDES OF ONE COIN?[1]

ABSTRACT

We find increasingly reservations about measuring success of societies by referring to GDP. Countering GDP-success-stories are not least the histories of personal failures and difficulties. Such histories are not about single items – as for instance poverty or discrimination – but reflect a multidimensional setting of issues that are in actual fact social concerns. As such, a composite assessment is needed that allows getting hold of the 'multidimensionality of exclusion'. For this, the work on the Anomie-index by the MTA provides an important instrument. However, it is also necessary to go beyond, finding a way to integrate this instrument into a wider methodological framework that allows understanding the social. The work on social quality refers to the social, as 'an outcome of the interaction between people (constituted as actors) and their constructed and natural environment. Its subject matter refers to people's interrelated productive and reproductive relationships.' *(van der Maesen/Walker, 2012; here: 260).* With this we propose an approach that provides indicators which are by definition going beyond measuring instruments.

INTRODUCTION

In general history is seen as somewhat slow process, things only changing at a snail's pace, fundamental structures remaining in place even if there are some changes on the surface. If we acknowledge the relevance of some quick changes and occasionally quick 'fixes' on the *niveau événementielle,* the more fundamental discourses on meaning, perspectives and the 'how to live and what life is about' appear as matter of even the *longue durée.* However, apparently we find currently a shift of the focus that contradicts such view: within a more or less short period of time we can find some major turns of debates in social science: after an increasing awareness of the shortcomings of modernist approaches to development as for instance those put forward in sociological terms by Toennies and Parsons or as matter of economics by Smith, Keynes or Rostow *(for the critique of such approaches*

---

[1] Notes made in preparation of a presentation of the Hungarian Academy of Science, June 12th, 2014

see e.g., the 'Atkinson report' [Atkinson/Cantillon/Marlier/Nolan, 2002]; the EU-Commission's debate on growth beyond GDP,[2] *not least in connection with criticising poverty debates etc.; of course, the Human Development Reports;*[3] *also the work of the Commission on the Measurement of Economic Performance and Social Progress, chaired by Joseph Stiglitz, Amartya Sen acting as chair-advisor and Jean-Paul Fitoussi acting as coordinator*[4]*),* we find now a shift towards anomie – for instance in Budapest with the work of Ference Bódi and team at the MTA and of course in general in connection with the debates around austerity politics and policies, environmental hazards and the like. However, it is important to acknowledge that these debates are part of a more fundamental critique of the *Zeitgeist,* which emerged not least against the backdrop of the system change: instead of the 'End of History' *(Fukujama),* we actually face a new beginning:[5] the transformation of parts of the world (the former communist countries, Asia, Latin America) confronts us with questions about the price we are asked to pay for the transformation. The *previous historical phase* had been to a large extent characterised by a fundamentally optimistic stance – though problems had not necessarily been denied, it had been suggested that they would be temporally and regionally limited. However, the limits to growth, heading environmental concerns in the 1970 *(Meadows, 1972)* are now seen within a much broader scope, concerned with a fundamentally pessimistic outlook, understood as matter of environmental, economic/financial and socio-cultural issues, i.e., a lack of overall sustainability.

In this light it is decisive to note the interlocution of different dimensions:

- A long-term orientation of analysis and critique goes hand in hand with short-term orientations
- The orientation on the objective conditions, as matter of living conditions and as well as matter of productive processes, goes hand in hand with the orientation on questioning values and meaning
- The concern with 'environmental sustainability' is fundamentally interwoven with issues of the quality of life and 'La Qualità Umana' *(Peccei, 1977)* – in this anthropocentric way always in danger of an instrumentalist approach to nature and also an individualist approach to existence.

Characteristically, Paul Boccara speaks of a *crise anthroponomique (Boccara, 2010, 2012)* which he explores as systematic crisis, i.e., 'une crise du système économique et également du système anthroponomique, c'est-à-dire du système qui concerne toute la vie humaine en dehors de l'économie, avec ses quatre moments : le parental, le travail, le politique et l'informationnel (la connaissance, la culture).' *(Ivorra, 2013: 3)*

[2] http://ec.europa.eu/environment/beyond_gdp/index_en.html - 09/06/2014

[3] http://hdr.undp.org/en - 09/06/2014

[4] see for the work and also for the report www.stiglitz-sen-fitoussi.fr - 25/12/2010 10:56 a.m. – see on the critique of the latter for instance Herrmann, 2012

[5] Though Fukuyama maintains his view; *see e.g., Fukuyama 2015.*

ANOMIE AND SOCIAL QUALITY – IN SEARCH FOR NEW METHODOLOGICAL GUIDELINES

Although we surely have to respect the concerns of public debates as new, we should not forget that we also face a kind of circular reoccurrence of these debates. Outstandingly, Emile Durkheim (1858 – 1917) pointed in his work on the problematique of anomie. We can summarise that in his view the crucial point had been the mismatch between different organisational and integrative principles of society. He discussed it mainly as unsolvable tension between organic and mechanical integration. Robert K. Merton furthered this approach in his work on Social Structure and Anomie *(Merton, 1938).* He contends 'that certain phases of social structure generate the circumstances in which infringement of social codes constitutes a 'normal' response.' *(ibid.: 672)* His point of reference is the congruity between 'culturally defined goals, purposes, and interests' *(ibid.)* and 'institutional norms' *(ibid.: 673)* as matters of regulation. I tried together with Claire Dorrity to grasp the issue in a different and wider way by relating appropriation and equality to each other *(see Herrmann/Dorrity, 2009: 14).* There it is referred to

> *points in which the social and individual actions merge with each other. Each of them have two dimensions:*
>
> - *appropriateness as*
>   - *'availing of property'*[6] *and*
>   - *adequacy and*
> - *equality as*
>   - *contestable legitimacy ('control of the system') and*
>   - *empowerment in terms of developing capabilities ('control of the own life and development')*
>
> *The tensions and options are as follows:*

		appropriation	
		property	adequacy
equality	legitimacy		
	empowerment		

Figure 6. Scope of Social Production.

[6] Not to be confused with property formation under private law.

(see as well Herrmann, 2014 b: 92 ff.). The proposed re-interpretation allows as well moving away from the psychological interpretation that is inherent in the Durkheimian thinking. We may refer to Robert Castel's reading of Locke, actually geared to establish an immediate connection between the psychological and soci(et)al level of ownership, and the level of praxis and legal status. For him the establishment a material basis of independence or autonomy paradoxically establishes at the very same time, uno actu, sovereignty as the reference to Kant – 'À ce modèle Locke oppose celui de l'indépendance, que l'on pourrait traduire philosophiquement dan le lange de Kant comme « l'autonomie de la volonté ». …' *(Castel, 2001 : 15)* – suggests as well the acknowledgement of the categorical imperative as suggested in the Critique of Practical Reason.

However, going back to Durkheim and Merton, the 'dissolution paradigm' – mechanic vs. organic solidarity – lacks sufficient differentiation and is at the end actually somewhat static *(see also Herrmann, 2009).* Furthermore, Durkheim and Merton alike do not discuss or question the 'normality of the system', thus being one-sided in their consideration of the social dimension. As explicitly stated in the beginning of Merton's work, it is about the nonconformity of individuals, not giving space to nonconformity of the system and the interpretation of development as matter of processing, i.e., permanently ongoing socialisation – a process that always changes its own foundations and conditions. In other words, nonconformity occurs on the side of individuals and of social entities alike. The reference to Castel's interpretation of property would open such perspective.

Also, more promising is the reference to a more developmentalist approach – a first point of reference can be seen in the work of Kondratieff and the bol'shie tsiklys, i.e., major cycles and the respective discussion that followed his proposals. The aim of the present interpretation is to suggest two things:

- developing a truly developmental perspective
- bringing (political) economy back on the agenda and linking it thoroughly to social quality thinking.

This means also to push social quality thinking further, working on the meaning of structure, structuration and change of political economy (as reality of the political economy and the analysis alike). It requires going beyond the standard interpretation of the 'major cycles' *(see the works by Nikolai Kondratieff, Carlota Perez and Daniel Šmihula),* not least establishing strong links to other paradigms. Especially the work of Daniel Šmihula *(Šmihula, 2011)* is promising as he aims on developing a wider perspective, although he maintains the primarily technologically based interpretation of development.[7]

In any case, social quality and anomie analysis alike are only meaningful if they are undertaken against the background of the overall shift of the conditions from which they emerge – this is the reason for proposing a strong reference to matters of the economy in a wide understanding, namely as matter of production and reproduction of people's daily life.

This will make it fruitful to interpret the approach to major cycles with help of a systematic combination of the following approaches and paradigms:

[7] There is as well some debate that proposes applying the long waves paradigm directly to political development which will not be taken up here.

- an extended understanding of the French theory of regulation, looking at the accumulation regime and mode of regulation and exploring from there specific living regimes and modes of life – part of this has to take the debate on the varieties of capitalism into account although those debates are reductionist in two ways: (a) they are commonly only concerned with the micro level and (b) the proposed degree of variation is in fact extremely limited.
- World Systems Theory, allowing to understand the social division of labour on a global level
- the distinction and drawing together of the different moments of the process of production, namely production in the strict sense, consumption, distribution and exchange – this can be seen as matter of accumulation regime and living regime
- and not least Karl Polanyi's approach is important, distinguishing between reciprocity, distribution and market as mechanisms of steering and – not less important – he discusses the embeddedness of economic activities – this can be seen as matter of mode of regulation and mode of life.

Resulting from this attempt to draw together different approaches, waiting for its further elaboration, we can also discuss social quality and anomie in a new light, the latter being of special interest here.

THE ATTRACTION OF THE TOPIC

As said in the outline, anomie is very much a recurrent topic. However, explicitly re-issuing it is a more recent matter – with a broad brush it can be linked to the processes of inclusion. As such, anomie is very much a specific form of failed inclusion. Importantly, we are not talking about inclusion of individuals. Instead, at stake is the failure of society to provide necessary mechanisms that translate simple inclusion into integration, understood in the twofold way of integrating people (as individuals and groups) and as establishing itself as integrated entity. One of the major conditions for this potential – and at times actual – structural tension is the increasingly inclusive character of society *(see Herrmann, 2014 a).*

This problematique, however, is in tendency already topic in various ancient social thoughts. We may first refer to Ancient Greek philosophy where Aristotle juxtaposes chrematistike and oikonomia, only the latter being concerned with an integrated system. The character of work under the condition of an economy that is developed in terms of having differentiated structures of production and distribution is important for the present context. In other words we are looking at the tension between an 'original state' of completely integrated socio-economic systems on the one hand and on the other hand a differentiated system which is characterised by (i) the tendency to develop a distinct economic sphere and (ii) the tendency to increase the distance between production of goods and the reproduction of daily life. The way in which a society deals with this tension is decisive when it comes to defining the scope and mode of social integrity.

We may equally point on Asian traditions where the tension had been also overcome by exclusion. The 'original state' had been about the good life for a few, taking wealth for granted and not allowing to question its existence, not asking from where it came. –

Especially the Confucian tradition of the special esteem granted to the bureaucratic classes can be seen as evidence for this – this had been a class of non-working people, perhaps we may even call them parasites, at the same time the link to the state bureaucracy showing the different meaning of 'individuality' *(see van der Maesen, 2012: 2 f.)*.

Looking at structural aspects and their economic foundation, we are concerned with a two-dimensional process.

The one is concerned with a secular process of inclusion – of course, suggesting this at a time where the topic of exclusion and incurring inequality is topical, may sound cynical. However, if we look unprejudiced at the long-term development we can see easily processes of increasing inclusion along different lines:

- the line of 'social' inclusion, i.e., the inclusion in terms of overcoming stratification – this does not suggest complete inclusion, but is a matter of moving the processes and structures of differentiation and segregation into society *(see e.g., the discussion on development of rights – see Marshall, 1950, see also Bulmer/Rees (eds.), 1996)*
- the line of 'spatial' inclusion, i.e., the increasing knowledge and use of space 'beyond immediate reach'
- the line of 'natural' inclusion, i.e., the inclusion of 'nature' and the 'environment' into the social processes
- the line technical inclusion, i.e., the fact that technology is increasingly an immediate part of daily life.

The other process evolves around the process Karl Polanyi elaborated in his opus magnum as matter of disembedding. Here we find the following moments, namely

- the separation within the process of production, namely the increasing intermediarisation;
- with this we see the separation of production and consumption – this is also and not least changing the character of consumption, separating it increasingly from the reproductive process itself;
- the change of the reproductive process by way of an increasing mediatisation, i.e., the 'meaning' of consumption does not come from the satisfaction immediately linked to the goods but the attributed societal meaning (positional goods etc.);
- however, the societal dimension itself is not a unilateral structure; instead, it is a matter of complex structural processing (in social science this had been variously discussed, by way of proposing developmental models (as the development 'from status to contract') or by way of proposing a new theoretical understanding of structure – e.g., Giddens proposes the concept of 'structuration' *(Giddens, 1984)*, Archer speaks of conflation *(Archer 1988; 1995; 2000; Archer 2003)*, and Slife proposes ontological relationality *(Slife, 2004)*. The social quality approach suggests two dialectical tensions that determine the social, namely the one between societal and biographical processes, the other between institutional and community structures. The overall 'architecture' is presented in the following overviews, the first presenting the two fundamental lines of dialectical tensions.

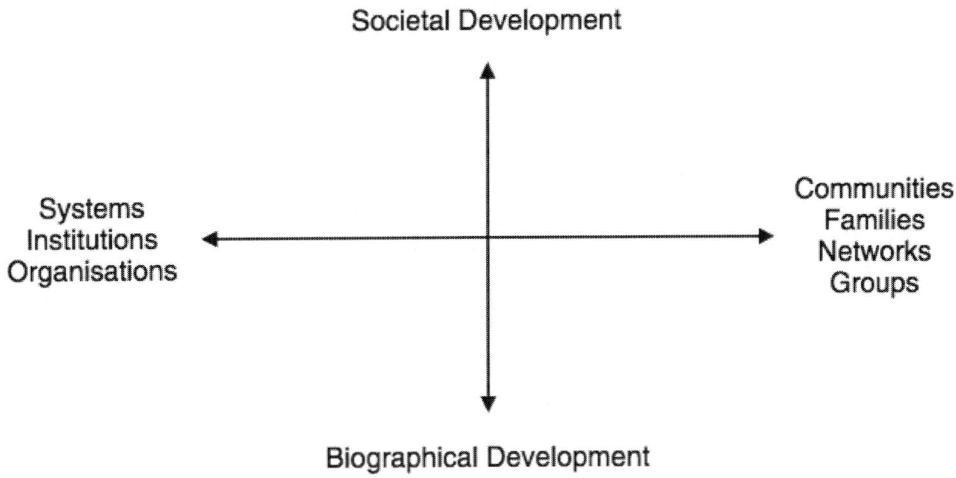

(from: Beck/van der Maesen/Walker, 2012: 51)

Overview 1. Interplay between two basic tensions.

Within this framework, a set of 3 by 4 factors is applied – these are outlined in the following:

Constitutional factors *(processes)*	***conditional factors*** *(opportunities + contingencies)*	***normative factors*** *(orientation)*
personal (human) security	*socio-economic security*	*social justice (equity)*
social recognition	*social cohesion*	*solidarity*
social responsiveness	*social inclusion*	*equal value*
personal (human) capacity	*social empowerment*	*human dignity*
profiles as instruments to analyse the change of the nature of these factors	*indicators as instruments to analyse the change of the nature of these factors*	*ethical based criteria for deepening and understanding these factors*

(van der Maesen, 2012: 4).

Overview 2. The Social Quality Architecture – Relevant Factors.

It should be considered to add a further set of conditional factors, namely factors that are – at least for the time being – completely out of control of the relevant actors. (Socio-)Natural disasters are one example, another may be trade embargos.

At least for the conditional (see Overview 3) and constitutional (see Overview 4) factors we can also show the relevant allocation in the tensional field which provides a framework for determining the social.

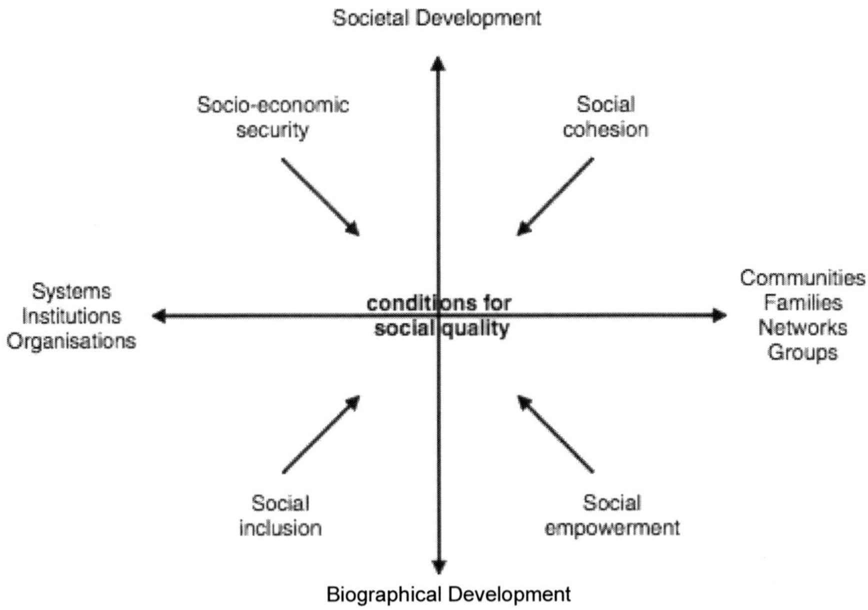

(Beck/van der Maesen/Walker, 2012: 61).

Overview 3. The Quadrangle of the Conditional Factors.

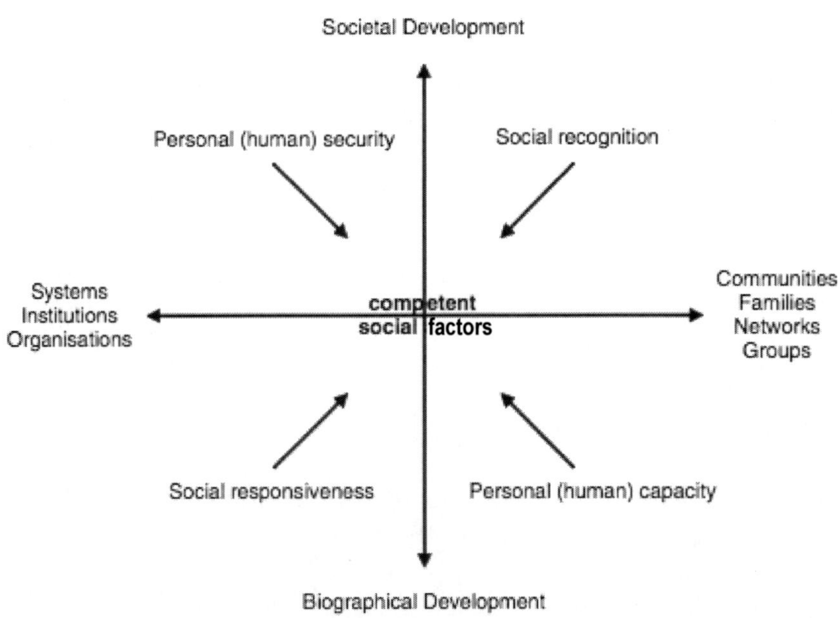

(ibid.: 57).

Overview 4. The Quadrangle of the Constitutional Factors.

ANOMIE AND SOCIAL QUALITY

The present contribution proposes that this elaboration can also serve as guideline for discussing methodologically both, anomie and social quality in terms of a possible systematic link between the two.

First, a common misunderstanding in respect of both, social quality and anomie needs urgently to be addressed: both should not be taken as valuation. In particular in the conceptualisation of SQ there had been at the early stage a suggestion that speaking of social quality implies the meaning of 'high' quality. However, quality is a categorical term, referring to a methodological level, allowing different manifestations.

Second, though both are categorical in character, the level they address is rather different. (Social) Quality means to address a higher level of abstraction whereas anomie is directed to a specific level of disintegration. The following levels are suggested:

	FUNDAMENTAL QUESTION THAT IS ADDRESSED	SPECIFIC QUESTION THAT IS ADDRESSED	MAIN ORIENTATION AND REFERENCE	OVERALL AIM/OUTCOME
SQ	mechanisms of societal integration	defining and characterising the quality of the social	processuality any relationality	analysis of trends and suggestion of political strategies
A	mechanisms of individual integrity	characterising mechanisms of disintegration	structures	analysis of status and suggestion of structural changes

Overview 5. Orientation of Anomie and Social Quality Research in a Comparative Perspective.

A first implication concerns the subject matter. The social quality approach is concerned with defining the social by providing an analytical tool to develop a clear understanding of what the social is – as such it is oriented on analysing complex relationships that are geared to everyday's life as matter of processes of production and reproduction. Furthermore, it allows to understand these relationships as matter of the interaction of the micro- and macro-level *(actually this formulation is already problematic though such distinction is only possible as heuristically relevant, but not relevant by way of suggesting methodological individualism or as matter of methodological socialism [see the contribution* World Systems Theory and Theory of Social Quality as Proposal for a Methodology for Rethinking a World in Crisis and Transformation *on pages 112 ff. of the present volume]. Finally, it allows developing a systematic understanding of the relationality of economic and non-economic factors (for this purpose it had been earlier suggested to include the reference to the French school of regulationists into the methodological orientation).*

On the other hand, anomie is referring to the 'disintegration' of some form of an integrated entity, however, without providing a sufficiently developed tool to understand what this entity is about, i.e., without defining the framework of reference. – Part of the problem is that Durkheim approached the question from both, a sociological and a socio-psychological perspective.

Third, sustainability is intrinsically part of the social quality approach as one of the cornerstones is processuality. Thus we find as well a developmental perspective: we may characterise social quality as realist-transcending: the realist part is the concern with people's everyday's life as matter or productive and reproductive relationships. Furthermore, the realist part is the inclusion of the constructed and natural environment. However, we also find a 'transcending aspect', insofar the social quality approach aims on structural changes not simply of the status quo but furthermore of the developmental model. Important are both, how the social as core reference is actually defined and the architecture used as analytical framework for analysing societal trends and developing policy recommendations. The underlying definition of the social is providing a major challenge of any analysis, not least when it comes to empirical studies. The social is understood as 'an outcome of the interaction between people (constituted as actors) and their constructed and natural environment. Its subject matter refers to people's interrelated productive and reproductive relationships.' *(van der Maesen/Walker, 2012: 260)*

In conclusion, if we talk about 'high' social quality as matter of development, considering the environment as genuine part of the social and vice versa, social relationships as immediate part of the environment,[8] we arrive at seeing sustainability as the only option and moreover as integral issue, philosophically speaking: as element. But we have to emphasise that sustainability is not simply about maintaining a status quo. An attempt to answer the challenge is the following: at stake is securing the conditions that allow and guarantee the social at a qualitatively high standard. This marks the main difference also to anomie which deals only with the conditional factors, aiming on defining societal disintegration and lack of integrity hic et nunc.

There is a fourth fundamental moment: whereas the concept of anomie can be elaborated as analytical tool, allowing the characterisation of fractures, leading to a lack of sustainability (unsustainability), the social quality approach allows the determination of conditions needed for sustainability. This has nothing to do with 'positive thinking'; on the contrary it allows determining the *structural* aspects that hinder changing fundamentally the direction of processes. We have to highlight this difference: anomie, interpreted in this way, is more or less limited to a static equilibrium, aiming on establishing a 'balance between individuals and society', without questioning their character and without asking for a definition. In social quality terms we can see it as matter of fine-tuning of the conditional, constitutional and normative factors. On the other hand, social quality sees society and the social as fundamentally dynamic. We may even say: the social – as production and reproduction of everyday's life – is itself defined by change and movement, reaching from the simple process of the metabolism needed to maintain organic life to the complex forms of human and also human-organic-nature relationships.

Fifth, this means that the orientation of the two approaches is also different. On the one hand, social quality thinking is concerned with soci(et)al trends and their assessment whereas anomie can be geared towards measuring specific conditions. On the other hand it means that social quality action requires more fundamental changes as it is directed to macro-structural and micro-processual changes, i.e., changes concerned with societal as well as with biographical development and the interaction of these levels. Acting on anomie is however, in tendency geared to a linear approach, suggesting that changes on the macro-level are subsequently leading to changes on the level of individuals' living conditions.

This way, we may come to the overall conclusion that anomie is centrally concerned with the conditional factors of well-being. On the other hand, social quality is focused on the

[8] actually the term environment is already problematic, we should talk about something as vironment

constitutional factors by way of permanently changing fields of and for action. Furthermore, anomie as concept has the advantage of allowing measuring defects of integration, whereas social quality thinking is geared to developing tendencies towards (re-)shaping societies.

REFERENCES

Archer, Margaret S, 1988: *Culture and Agency: The Place of Culture in Social Theory*, Cambridge: Cambridge University Press.

Archer, Margaret S, 1995: *Realist Social Theory: the Morphogenetic Approach*, Cambridge: Cambridge University Press.

Archer, Margaret S, 2000: *Being Human: The Problem of Agency*, Cambridge University Press.

Archer, Margaret S, 2003: *Structure, Agency and the Internal Conversation*; Cambridge: Cambridge University Press.

Atkinson, Tony/Cantillon, Bea/Marlier, Eric/Nolan, Brian, 2002: *Social Indicators*. The EU and Social Inclusion; Oxford: Oxford University Press.

Beck, W./van der Maesen, L. J. G./Walker, A., 2012. Theoretical Foundations. In: van der Maesen, L.J.G/A. Walker (eds.), 2012: *Social Quality: From Theory to Indicators*. Basingstoke: Palgrave Macmillan. pp. 44–69.

Beck, Wolfgang/van der Maesen, Laurent/Walker, Alan, 2012: Theoretical Foundations; in: Social Quality. *From Theory to Indicators;* Laurent J.G. van der Maesen/Alan Walker (eds.); Houndsmills/New York: Palgrave MacMillan: 44-69.

Boccara, Paul, 2010: La crise systémique : une crise de civilisation. Ses perspectives pour avancer vers une nouvelle civilisation, note de la Fondation Gabriel Péri.

Boccara, Paul, 2012: Le Capital de Marx, son apport, son dépassement au-delà de l'économie; Paris : Le Temps des Cerises.

Bulmer, Martin/Rees, Anthony M. (eds.), 1996: *Citizenship Today*. The contemporary relevance of T.H. Marshall; London/Bristol: University of London Press.

Castel, Robert/Haroche, Claudine, 2001: Propriété Privée, Propriété Sociale, Propriété de Soi; Entretiens sur la Construction de l'Individu Moderne : Arthème Fayard.

Fukuyama, Francis, interview by Hiroyuki Nishimura, Nikkei, 2015: The end of history? America's fall from grace; in *Asian Review*; January 13, 2015 2:20 am JST; http://asia.nikkei.com/print/article/69716; 16/01/15.

Giddens, Anthony, 1984: *The Constitution of Society: Outline of the Theory of Structuration*; Oxford: Polity Press.

Herrmann, Peter, 2009: Gemeinschaft der Gesellschaft – die Suche nach einem Definitionsrahmen für Prekarität; in: Hepp, Rolf (ed.): The Fragilisation of Socio-structural Components/Die Fragilisierung soziostruktureller Komponenten; Bremen: *Europäische Hochschulschriften:* 76-107.

Herrmann, Peter, 2012: Economic Performance, Social Progress and Social Quality; in: *International Journal of Social Quality* 2(1), Summer: 41–55.

Herrmann, Peter, 2014 a: Precarity – An Issue of Changed Labour Market and Employment Patterns or of Changed Social Security Systems? in: Herrmann, Peter/Veredyuk, Olesya V./Bobkov, Viacheslav/Frangakis, Marica eds.: Labour M*arket and Precarity of*

Employment: general and specific in the Hungarian and Russia developments; Vienna: WVFS.

Herrmann, Peter, 2014 b: *Social Policy in Context*: Vienna WVFS.

Herrmann, Peter/Dorrity, Claire, 2009: Critic of Pure Individualism; in: Dorrity/Herrmann: Social Professional Activity: The Search for a Minimum Common Denominator in Difference; New York: Nova.

Ivorra, Pierre, 2013: Crise de civilisation, crise de 2008-2010 et solutions systémiques; in: Économie&Politique. Revue marxiste d'économie; 708-709, Juillet/Août 2013; 39-39.

Marshall, Tom H., 1950: Citizsenship and Social Class; in: Citizenship and Social Class; Tom H. Marshall/Tom Bottomore; London et altera: Pluto Press, 1992.

Meadows, Donella H., 1972: Limits to Growth?; Universe Books.

Merton, Robert K., 1938: Social Structure and Anomie; in: American Sociological Review; 3/5: 672-682.

Peccei, Aurelio, 1977: La Qualità Umana; Prefazione di Roberto Peccei, Introduzione di Gianfranco Bologna; Roma: Castelvecchi, 2014.

Slife, Brent F., 2004: Taking Practice Seriously: Toward a Relational Ontology; in: Journal of Theoretical and Philosophical Psychology; 24.2; 157-178.

Šmihula, Daniel, 2011: Long waves of technological innovations. «Long waves of technological innovations»; in: Studia Politica Slovaca [Studia Politica Slovaca], issue: 2 /2011, pages: 50-68, on www.ceeol.com; Electronic copy available at: http://ssrn.com/abstract=2353624.

van der Maesen, Laurent J.G., November 20th, 2012: Working-paper no 9: Elaboration of a Lecture on the Orientation, Strategies and Model (or Experiences) of the City of Hangzhou (Zhejiang province of mainland China), from a comparative; working papers at http://socialquality.eu/ - 20/09/2013.

van der Maesen, Laurent J.G./Walker, Alan, 2012: *Social Quality and Sustainability*; in: Van der Maesen, Laurent J.G./Walker, Alan (eds.): *Social Quality. From Theory to Indicators*: Basingstoke: Palgrave Macmillan; 250-274.

Part I. Scene XV: Gretchen's Room

(Gretchen alone at the spinning wheel.)
My peace is gone
My heart is sore:
I'll find it, never,
Oh, nevermore.
(197)

Chapter 5

World Systems Theory and Theory of Social Quality As Proposal for a Methodology for Rethinking a World in Crisis and Transformation[1]

Abstract

Two fundamental problems are standing at the outset of the following considerations:

- The current crisis is often seen as the deepest, longest lasting, fundamental etc.; however: it is not clearly spelt out that we are dealing with a truly systemic crisis, i.e., 'une crise du système économique et également du système anthroponomique, c'est-à-dire du système qui concerne toute la vie humaine en dehors de l'économie, avec ses quatre moments : le parental, le travail, le politique et l'informationnel (la connaissance, la culture).' *(Ivorra, 2013: 39; see also Boccara, 2010)*
- Globalisation is a nearly permanent point of reference in contemporary debates, however it is not clearly spelled out as something that is characterised by two very different dimensions which are actually to some extent contradicting each other: the one can be captured by an increasing density of relations between nation states and regions – the character of these may be very different; the other is a matter of the factually increased relational interdependence – and factual also means that the knowledge of this relational interdependence becomes a material force – alluding to *Karl Marx Critique of Hegel's Philosophy of Right (Marx, 1843/44: 180)* – very much like theory being appropriated by the masses.

The challenge is to find a proper analytical framework that allows taking both, the systemic character of the crisis and the globalisation of the current challenges in the second understanding of globalisation serious. Bringing World Systems Theory and Social Quality Theory together, provides a promising framework for finding an answer to present challenges.

[1] Preparations for a presentation for the workshop on Strategic Studies: Rethinking a World in Crisis and Transformation held by the Centro de Investigaciones de Política Internacional, Havana, October 2013

Inescapability of Globalisation

Looking at the current crisis in the said understanding of globalisation, it is obvious that highlighting its global character is not least linked to the fact that there is no escape possible: where previously economic development and crisis was characterised by apparent opportunities to 'externalise' unwanted moments in space and/or time, this is not possible anymore. Though there may be in some respect escapes still possible, this is more the exception than the rule. However, the reception of the crisis remains caught in national thinking – we may speak of methodological nationalism in the sense in which Maurice Roche coined the term, contending that analysis and politics 'are designed on a basis which appears to take the nation state, its sovereignty and the powers of its government utterly for granted.' *(Roche, 1992: 184 f.; quoted in Gore, 1996: 80)*

Gore himself goes further, pointing out

> Explanations which are methodologically nationalist try to explain economic and social trends in countries, basically reference to facts about the countries themselves. The focal object of understanding is often described as the economic or social 'performance' of a country, usually in comparison with other countries. Specific performances are typically 'explained' by dividing causal factors into 'internal' and 'external' factors, and then attributing what is happening in a single country or set of countries within a region of the world ... mainly to internal factors. (Gore, 1996: 80 f.)

This is a rather fundamental factor, in some way reaching further than aggressive nationalism and its internationalisation as imperialism. It is accepting theoretically and in ultimate terms of policy-making nationality as ultimate reason. Such approach of methodological nationalism actually reduces all debates on globalisation on international relationships, not allowing taking a cosmopolitical stance. This contradicts in a fundamental way the developmental stage of the means of production. It means also that it takes a wrong emphasis on political processes and structures, neglecting the fundamental issue of political economy. The nation state had been seedbed and result of the emergence of capitalism. With capitalism reaching obviously its structural limits, we have to open the view also in terms of the framework of regulation – and we all know that this is already happening in different ways: World Bank, IMF, UN etc. are just few examples – showing the general need and also the limitations characterising the current situation.

Moving this argument further we face in very general terms following, in part contradicting, patterns.

(i) Local reference of production proper (with its four elements: manufacturing, consumption, distribution and exchange) does not play a decisive role. Importantly this includes the increasing relevance of locality: the number of small traders, the orientation on local consumption etc. are growing hand in hand with the number and spread of large corporations.

(ii) Based on different mechanisms, we find in terms of the mode of production developments pointing in opposite directions: large scale, automated production is standing side by side with an again increasing small-scale, craftsmanship guided work.

(iii) Notwithstanding the fact of global dominance of the capitalist mode of production, we see that the prevailing non-capitalist elements are currently regaining relevance also in quantitative terms:

- the increasing meaning of work disfavouring labour
- increasing meaning of direct exchange and even of use-value exchange, not replacing market-mediated forms but complementing them in certain areas beyond the 'neighbourly help' that is already well known as epiphenomenon of capitalism
- increasing meaning of 'direct provisions' both as direct provision of statutory services and as 'charitable welfare'
- also in the political sphere we find increasingly signs of a shift beyond the patterns of democratic-national policy production; this is not primarily about the increasing meaning of supra- and international bodies – more important is the loss of demos as at least formally acknowledged point of reference and actor.[2]

(iv) With this we find another contradictory pattern, namely the fact that on the one hand economics takes globally completely over, penetrating all pores of life, however meaning at the same time that any development, and with this any crisis, is also a systemic crisis, already earlier defined as 'une crise du système économique et également du système anthroponomique, c'est-à-dire du système qui concerne toute la vie humaine en dehors de l'économie, avec ses quatre moments : le parental, le travail, le politique et l'informationnel (la connaissance, la culture).' *(Ivorra, 2013: 39)*

Change As System Change – Change As Systemic Change

Not only the crisis points on the systemic instability – perhaps even more the persistence of systemic alternatives is proof of this fact. Admittedly, the 'great revolution' is at least for the time being lost – it is not the occasion to fully discuss the details. A short note, however, is required: In my understanding one of the major problems was not a 'political failure'; nor do we have to blame primarily the 'economic strength of the West'. Instead we have to investigate to which extent this search for alternatives was really a matter of dealing with the entire and complex mode of production with all the different aspects of manufacturing, consumption, distribution and exchange as relationship of elementary forms of society building, i.e., the entity of accumulation regime, mode or regulation, living regime and mode of life. This brings me to the two main analytical dimensions that I want to suggest for both, analysis and developing a perspective for future politics and policies.

World Systems Theory

The positive side of World Systems Theory is that it provides a framework that allows *thorough* consideration of the complexity of relationships between states and regions,

[2] This is in actual facto a far-reaching statement, suggesting policy making as process of production that follows similar patterns as capitalist commodity production.

considering these not least as power relationships, going far beyond recently increased and accelerated 'trade relations'. And of utmost importance is the fact that World Systems Theory draws our attention to hegemonic relations: capitalism as dominant system, though structuring dominance, ruling and governance in highly complex and differentiated ways. Important is not least the fact that hegemony also means the differentiated involvement of those who are object of processes of ruling into the systems of ruling (governance).

Though the related debates are varied when it comes to details, it should be said that the differentiated view on the actual mode of production – going beyond a rough formative perspective – remained by and large limited. We may speak of 'methodological capitalism', not sufficiently allowing the view on a world system in which capitalism does not exist or is not dominant. Even the link between hegemonic centres and subordinated periphery is not sufficiently analysed by way of thoroughly considering differences in the modes of production *(see already page 57)*. The present proposal – which surely needs further elaboration – emphasises that any mode of production is in actual fact a composition of different moments. Broadly we may say that one dimension consists of the four elementary forms of production, namely production (A), consumption (B), distribution (C) and exchange (D).

The other dimension is based on the contradictory aspects that were mentioned earlier. It is schematised in the conceptual form of considering spatiality and time-comprehensiveness of production (1), economies of scale (2), value dimension of production [priority of use or exchange value] (3) and political-economic governance (4).

Lacking a better term, I propose to classify each of them by their 'degree of modernity'.[3] This translates into the following meanings of 'developed stages'

(1) national boundary, oriented on competitiveness
(2) large scale, 'industrial' production
(3) dominance of exchange value, disfavouring use value
(4) rational and bureaucratic rule of law.

We have to consider a further step, namely the application of these dimensions on (at least) two levels, i.e., the national (or possibly regional) level (I) and the international level (II).

Bringing this together, allows us presenting the following scheme.

	1		2		3		4	
	I	II	I	II	I	II	I	II

Matrix 8. Analytical Scheme for Assessing Countries.

[3] 'Modernity' in the present understanding is by no means understood as simply a progressive and positive pattern or stage of development. Instead, here it is simply a 'descriptive' means, capturing the pattern of societal organisation that developed with the contradictions as result of the bourgeois revolution and Western-style enlightenment.

This may be also seen as foundation for an empirical analysis of a global order, classifying dependencies. It can be used to calculate a weighted index that comprises the different countries and regions on the basis of their share in performance values. However, importantly we have to recognise that the valuation and weighting has two dimensions: the one is the simple calculation of relevant values; more difficult is however determining the qualitative aspect. Taking the given historical stage this is of crucial meaning. In a nutshell: we see that many of the standards are breaking away and that hegemonic claims cannot be made on the same foundations which had been unquestioned for a long time: growth of GDP as standard measuring wealth, economies of scale, locality and identity … – these are just few examples marking shifts on the scale of valuation of the foundation of hegemonic claims.

Social Quality Theory

This leads directly to the argument that social quality is actually not just an attractive paradigm. Instead we find a proposal that is geared towards rethinking a world in crisis and transformation.

that the argument is that World Systems Theory is in some way only a formal framework, considering an important and even central aspect of societal constitution of which Frederick Engels said that

> [a]ccording to the materialist conception, the determining factor in history is, in the last resort,, the production and reproduction of immediate life. But this itself is again of a twofold character. On the one hand, the production of the means of subsistence, of food, clothing and shelter and the implements required for this; on the other, the production of human beings themselves, the propagation of the species. The social institutions under which men of a definite historical epoch and of a definitive country live are determined by both kinds of production: by the stage of development of labour, on the one hand, and of the family on the other. (Engels, 1884: 131)

Only if we recognise the complex points made by Engels, we will be able to elaborate the substantial side which World Systems Theory fails to develop. Of course, classical Marxist analysis left a large part of the social dimension outside of its immediate consideration, not least by implicitly developing it by providing a methodological framework.

- A shortcoming, however, has to be seen in the fact that the classical Marxist approach was limited by focusing the analysis on the emerging capitalist formation – suggesting this way a very specific take on social issues.[4]
- Furthermore, leaving few exceptions aside, the idea of ‘one society’ did actually not exist – instead, class society as divided society was ‘accepted reference’. ‘Hegemony’, in this respect, was only spelled out as blunt ruling of market force: oppression, hierarchy, dependency, living at the margins … – all this had been by and large unquestioned and did not need much of justification by pretending harmony. The divided society had been given and it had been suggested as ‘natural

[4] Given by the need of thinking about issues concerned with securing matters of mere existence.

order'. As it had been a reinterpretation of the 'liberal citizen-society', the revolution of the citoyenitée was a failed project which had been maintained regardless of its massive shortcomings: It was a failed project as it did not keep its promises of equality and fraternity; however, it stayed on the agenda by promising ongoing liberty, though reduced on freedom of the agents on the market. In this sense the paradox was that a highly unequal society that could justifiably claim to be the heir of the anti-feudalist revolution.

- As much as the 'project capitalist formation' was caught by and limited in the framework of a utilitarian project, the adjunct 'social project' remained caught by the same limitation: as the one was very much guided by methodological nationalism, the other was very much based in methodological individualism. Both moved in the very same framework. For the 'social project' it meant for instance pedagogisation, psychologisation, 'securitisation', and 'provisionalisation' (granting of benefits and services) and the like.
- This meant not least that thinking (about) the social was limited by the extent to which a perspective that would be able to transcend presence as time frame and nation state as space was developed. Furthermore, it limited in this way the social perspective on an 'add-on', not able to present a truly genuine understanding of the social.

The social quality theory emerged in the middle of the 1990s in order to argue in favour of a more social Europe. However, being in the beginning very much concerned with a rebuke of 'economistic over-determination', it became increasingly clear that the problem is not a supposed dominance of the economic sphere. Instead, the problem was increasingly seen as a lack of the definition of the social – understood as noun. In general, social science refers to the social without even thinking about its underlying substance – substituting considerations by reference to supposed aggregates (as society, state etc.) or to assumed attributes of values and moral characteristics. Analysing social situations in this light was usually rather short-sighted, being on the one hand concerned with institutional perspectives of provisions of socio-economic security (pensions, health care, social benefits ...), looking on the other hand at ethical and moral dimensions of behaviour. The SQT, however, looks at the social, understood as noun and defined as 'an outcome of the interaction between people (constituted as actors) and their constructed and natural environment. Its subject matter refers to people's interrelated productive and reproductive relationships. In other words, the constitutive interdependency between processes of self-realisation and processes governing the formation of collective identities is a condition for the social and its progress or decline.' *(van der Maesen/Walker, 2012: 260)*

The definition resulted from an iterative approach – which had been originally limited to EUropean member states.[5]

It is based in three sets of factors, namely: conditional factors, constitutional factors and normative factors, defined by four dimensions each. We arrive at the following architecture, determining the social and allowing to assess its quality.

[5] Due to the origin of the work and the availability of funding

Constitutional factors *(processes)*	***conditional factors*** *(opportunities + contingencies)*	***normative factors*** *(orientation)*
personal (human) security	*socio-economic security*	*social justice (equity)*
social recognition	*social cohesion*	*solidarity*
social responsiveness	*social inclusion*	*equal value*
personal (human) capacity	*social empowerment*	*human dignity*
profiles as instruments to analyse the change of the nature of these factors	*indicators as instruments to analyse the change of the nature of these factors*	*ethical based criteria for deepening and understanding these factors*

(van der Maesen, November 20th, 2012: 4).

As said, so far the concept was originally developed by way of collaborating colleagues from EU-member states, and later it had been further discussed with colleagues from different Asian countries.

All this is surely still work in progress – at this stage the following major challenges can be made out:

- to integrate rights-based thinking, and this is also a matter of legal paradigms, into the theory;
- to develop a clearer economic thinking in this context, i.e., developing social quality thinking further in connection with political economy is a more urgent task;
- to globalise the approach, i.e., to go beyond its application in different countries and regions and to adapt the general scaffold to the conditions en lieu: at the end – and linking to what had been said – we always have been and are increasingly visible and palpable for everybody – living in one global world: not 'interconnected nation states' but one space, defined by the same conditions, challenges, practices and futures;
- to 'communitarise' the approach by looking at concrete ways in which people accommodate their lives in the given circumstances.

Social quality in this brief outline will provide a useful guideline and framework for the envisaged research. However, a clearer understanding requires entering a wider array of paradigms that should at least be briefly mentioned as complementing SQT and SQA, allowing at least to arrive at a clearer understanding of the context in which developments of societies, the social and identity stand today. It is important that this approach actually focuses on two ends. On the one hand it has to stand against national or spatial boundaries. This can be summarised by two contentions, presenting the political and the economic perspective. Hans Heinrich Rupp states that 'thinking in spatial categories is the enemy of all academic legal attempts to conceive of law as a social phenomenon' *(Rupp, 1991: 258 – translation P.H.).* And Philip E. Steinberg emphasise the economic dimension, contending that 'the territorial state emerged concurrent with the deterritorialization of political economy and geographical imagination' *(Steinberg, 2009: 468).*

On the other hand, however, it emphasises the ultimate importance of the community level as place of immediate interaction and with this the (re-)production of the social. This is not least an answer on the dissolution of boundaries we face in the current socio-political economy: Social space, i.e., the spaces in which people interact amongst themselves and with the organic environment in a given timeframe – on another occasion I presented this as spacetime *(Herrmann, 2013).* Seeing overcoming this dissolution as serious challenge is urgently needed in order to address more seriously the question of sustainability as social, spatial and temporal borrowing.

MONDIALIST HUMANISM

An optimistic reading suggests so far that we are able to refer to a methodological framework – perhaps we may even claim two frameworks: one of methodological mondialism and the other of methodological socialism – allowing us to *analyse* the current situation fairly well. Furthermore, it is also a framework that is relatively open to different ideological approaches. *Relatively* means it takes openly position towards the political goal of a *world* society that provides equal opportunities for all – a formula that brings together the three sets of factors; but within this broad remit it recognises the need to accept different traditions, different structural patterns and set-ups and different concrete political processes coming to the fore as strategic perspectives.

The, for me, most important point is that we reached a historical turning point that bears some similarities with the situation to which Karl Marx referred, claiming that '[a]t a certain stage of development it brings forth the material agencies for its own dissolution. From that moment new forces and new passions spring up in the bosom of society; but the old social organisation fetters them and keeps them down.' *(Marx, 1867: 749)*

To use Antonio Gramsci's expression, this crisis is a phase where 'the old is dying and the new cannot be born' *(passim).* Seemingly – at first glance – this contests both, many aims we were striving for in reformist and revolutionary attempts and many achievements reached during the historical development of the last 150 plus years: social insurance, social benefits, even human rights in the understanding of mainstream interpretations. This means, however, only to recognise fully the historical character of society and the social.

I have to limit myself on highlighting few fields that I see as cntral under the heading of the search for international humanitarian law.

(1) We actually have to go beyond the search for humanitarian law, and reclaim demanding true human rights
(2) We have to develop anti-imperialism by way of moving towards genuine mondialism[6]
(3) We have to search for ways overcoming 'social provisionalism' by enabling soci(et)al self-determination
(4) We have to find ways of re-naturalising the mode of production, re-installing it as conscious metabolism.

---

[6] This term is taken to differentiate the process from globalisation, the latter describing only an intensified relationship between nation states. – In this context I am grateful for discussions with Paul Boccara and Bruno Amoroso.

Ad 1

There is a certain shortcoming if we speak of humanitarian law.

- Though the term *humanitarian* suggests intuitively an emphasis on *relations* between human beings, founded in mutual respect,[7] it suggests also a 'soft' understanding of such respect and egalitarianism. In this respect, reference to human beings has a stronger recognition of respecting human existence in its own right.
- The important relationality, i.e., complex of relations between human beings – is regained by orienting on rights. With this we are overcoming some structural limitations of law which tend to reduce dealings on formalised relations between individuals.

Such orientation would not least mean to orient strongly on the right to self-determined (re-)production in terms of

- determining use-values, instead of being determined by exchange values; this includes importantly the recognition of the (re-)production of social relations as productive force;
- optimising relationships to – or better: their integration into – 'nature', i.e., a determined respect of collective rights within a given organic environment; this can be integrated into the proposal made by Durkheim by his analysis of mechanical solidarity.[8]

Taken together, this means that a human rights perspective has to develop towards a 4th generation: The right to collective (re-)productive self-determination, based on environmental integrity (see in this context the reference to collective group rights in the Bolivian Constitution[9] and the mutuality orientation of foreign policy inscribed into the Cuban Constitution).

The fundamental and far-reaching issue is the coming together of methodological individualism, methodological nationalism, methodological capitalism and methodological hierarchy-ism/zero-sum-orientation. As we are truly dealing with an indissoluble complexity, we are facing a methodological hurdle that is difficult to overcome.

First, the state and individuals are to a large extent separated from each other, the state acting 'on its own behalf'. It emerges on the one hand as instance of the ruling class.

However, second, using the term 'instance' instead of instrument means to acknowledge Poulantzas' quest for a differentiated view, highlighting 'that the state and its apparatuses constitute 'a relationship of forces, or more precisely the material condensation of such a relationship among classes and class fractions'' *(Schmalz/Ebenau, 2012: 490; quoting Poulantzas, 1978: 128 f.)*

But, third, at the same time it emerges as instance with its own 'proprium'. Nation sates – on the global level 'acting as individuals' *(here methodological nationalism and*

[7] always carrying an egalitarian notion with it

[8] In this light the term 'organic' environment refers very much to the biological understanding of nature etc.

[9] not least as means of securing the right to self-determination of production

methodological individualism immediately merge) – compete with each other, arriving for the Commonwealth, understood as wealth of the nation which is at the end constituted on the basis of competitive advantage, and that means the cost of others *(here we see methodological capitalism and methodological hierarchism/zero-sum-assumption falling immediately together).*

This brings us then, fourth, finally to Joachim Hirsch's view on the 'competition state' *(Hirsch, 2005),* surely combining the states competitiveness with other states and the provision of conditions that allow enterprises to be nationally and internationally/globally competitive.

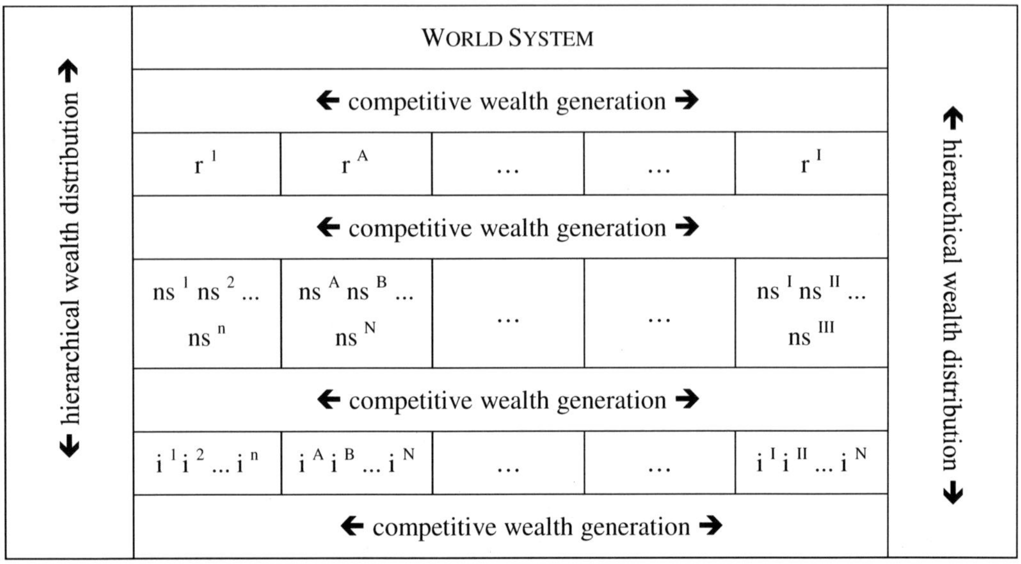

Overview 6. Wealth Generation and Distribution.

A paradoxical effect is occurring in various aspects.

- Human rights are limited to rights of taking part and place in global capitalism
- Global citizenship is easily limited to 'living ones nationality in different nations' *(cf. Bosniak, 2000).*
- (Re-)production is structurally limited to producing individual wealth in competition with others

> The most common diagnosis of the problem can be referred to, following John Kenneth Galbraith (1976), as the 'squirrel-wheel hypothesis.' According to this view, increased consumption does not generate lasting increments in welfare because the process of production itself generates new wants and needs. (Heath, 2000: 231; with reference to Galbraith, 1976)

This goes hand in hand with the question of competitive consumption in connection with the positional character of (some) goods.

> What makes the good in question 'nice' is its superiority to the plain one. Thus wanting to live in a house with nice things implicitly commits one to the logic of

competitive consumption, because as others acquire nice things as well, what was once nice becomes increasingly plain. (Heath, 2000: 233)

- We find a paradox insofar the 'escape' from the cage of the assumption of a zero-sum-game is given by a strategy of exponential growth, ironically only increasing the zero.

Ad 2

Seemingly contradicting is the second point, demanding a genuine mondialist perspective. Global competition and the orientation on competitiveness are as much in the way of such strategy as any attempt towards autarkic seclusion. This has especially major implications for international trade and taxation. Point of reference is ultimately a non-anthropocentric, non-present-time orientation. This means to see human existence as part of a much wider spectrum of existence: in question is indeed the universe and the possibility of the universal reproduction on a permanent (sustainable) basis. The rejection of anthropocentrism human existence does not escape the equation. In actual fact, human existence enters exactly at this point the stage by emphasising its existence as complex and concrete relation. Being 'part of' nature means that humans surely take parts out of nature (pars capere), but it also means that humankind can only exist within it and by securing its reproduction. Thus, securing these (inter-)dependencies is essential.

We are dealing with a specifically defined level of abstraction. On the one hand we are forced to look at a very concrete level of people's practice as '[r]elations are the most abstract and metaphysical ideas of any which men can have occasion to form, when they are considered by themselves and separated from the related object.' *(Blair, 1787: 0)*

However, on the other hand we are challenged to accept the concrete not simply as 'something given' but as something that is historically created and that can be changed. As Boaventura de Sousa Santos points out 'it is important not to reduce realism on what exists as doing so we would oblige oursel only to justify the existing, not withstanding how injustice and suppressing it may be.' *(Sousa Santos, 1997; translation P.H.)*

Ad 3

With this we arrive at a third point. Without tracing the line of historical development thoroughly back we can say that we reached a new stage on which human practice is divided in the following ways:

- One dividing line is going right through practice itself and defines economic activities as separate from the entirety of human practice. In the extreme we find this reflected in Marx' formulation on alienation, pointing on

the fact that labor is external to the worker, i.e.,, it does not belong to his intrinsic nature; that in his work, therefore, he does not affirm himself but denies himself, does not feel content but unhappy, does not develop freely his physical and mental energy but mortifies his body and ruins his mind. The worker therefore only feels himself outside his work, and in his work feels outside himself. He feels at home when he is not working, and when he is working he does not feel at home. (Marx, 1844: 274)

- Second, this establishes a central dividing line, juxtaposing human existence and human beings on the one hand and nature on the other. This is not about the freedom gained by knowing the laws of nature but about knowing the laws of nature in order to subordinate nature itself under humankind.
- With this we find as third dividing line the one between past, present and future. This is not as such a problem – the problem only begins where the need of continuity – as matter of working within the historical process – is denied and a loan is taken on the future without including considerations about how to pay this loan back.
- A fourth dividing line – to some extent bringing other lines together – concerns the regionally unequal distribution: though soci(et)al (re-)production is and will – objectively – always be a holistic process, it is artificially divided in respect of space and time: we borrow from other countries and from the future without considering the effects. And this means of course that some countries are lenders wheras some countries are donors. At this point terminological clarity is especially important. Though the rich countries may be indeed seen as donor countries in terms of money, they are actually only 'donating' by way of paying a kind of interest for the goods and services they receive. We can express this also in economic terms: parallel to the replacement of variable capital by constant capital, we find finance capital replacing real capital. Fact is, however, that the replacement of variable capital by constant capital ('rationalisation') can be structurally viable, the replacement of real capital by finance capital cannot. Actually this form of replacement ('f by r') is the attempt to maintain capitalism as 'virtual project'.

Here, the differentiation between real and fictive values, between natural and artificial wealth, between material and immaterial goods, between real and virtual economy does not make much sense. One could downright speak of a romanticist inverse profile (Verkehrungsprofil): the circulation of loans is based in the paradox of 'money that is reflexively guaranteed by itself' and proves to be a venue of effective fiction or 'seal', on the basis of which the circulation of the illusionary is emerging as determination of economic relations. (Vogl, 2010: 81 – translation PH)

- This is manifested in a fifth dividing line, actually itself a bundle of lines as between rural and urban areas, between the commodity producing Global South and the commodity consuming Global North, but increasingly between the global rich and the global poor.[10]

Of course, of crucial importance remains the class division, which finds also its prolongation and extension as part and parcel of the other divisions.

In actual fact, we are dealing with complex and interwoven processes of division: borrowing from the future and borrowing from other regions and borrowing from other

[10] Expressing the fact that there is an increasing wealth in so-called developing countries and the emergence of 'pockets' of poverty, precarity etc in the so-called developed countries.

classes and borrowing from nature are possibly temporarily advantageous – at least for one side. However, in the medium and especially long run such borrowing is not viable. Moreover, in the short and medium run it means facing an increasing limitation of the scope of action as soci(et)al practice is reduced on compensation by provision, not providing space for self-determination. – The debate on so-called developmental aid shows this throughout history again and again – even more: money, once spent, is in multiplied forms flowing back into the so-called donor countries. In any case, at the core stands the strict separation and moreover dissolution of entities where strategies of reintegration are prone to fail as long as the relational character is not acknowledged and matters are understood as being separate from each other, requiring to be welded together. The welding will only be successful if it starts from the original entity which has to be re-established on a higher level.

To the extent to which provisions are not part of the production itself, we face multiple dilemmas which can be summarised by saying that systems loose the capacities to reproduce themselves – this can be seen in the 'bubble-economies', demographic 'imbalances', environmental hazards, the fact that formal norms are overgrowing substantial rules, and not least the fact that 'productive potentials' are disregarded as they are not taking the commodity form. Many other features could be mentioned.

Demanding overcoming 'social-provisionalism', i.e., mechanisms of correcting soci(et)al ills by ex-post provisions, means in this light in simple terms moving towards a (re-) convergence of the various

- technical
- social
- temporal and
- spatial

moments of (re-)production.

In actual fact we are again returning to the importance of regional cultures of self-determined production.

Supposing a sufficiently wide understanding of the relevant terms and concepts (as e.g., technology), we arrive indeed at the question posed by Carlota Perez, who had been investigating if '[i]nnovation systems and policy are not only for the rich?' *(Perez, 2012).* Following the ideas of Kondratieff, she sees the following patterns emerging:

> Mass production needed the dumbing-down of the workers in order for management to define the 'one best way'. This was the price to pay for getting the high productivity that made possible turning the blue collar workers into middle income consumers. It was low quality of life at work and high quality outside work. By contrast, flexible production, to achieve best results, needs to use the creativity and imagination of all personnel.19 The consequence could be high quality of life at work and at home, if knowledge and participation are adequately rewarded. (ibid.: 10; with reference to Lorenz/Lundvall 2011)

Leaving the details aside, the challenge will indeed be to explore the potential of the perspective means of production to go beyond an increase of productivity, reaching a spread of outcome in two perspectives:

- benefitting the producers and
- understanding production as process that is oriented on producing 'the social' of a high quality.

On another occasion *(e.g., Herrmann, 2010: 268),* I provided a *Tentative Comparative Outlook on Asia – Europe* in respect of the mode of societal production, the mode of societally constituting distribution and the mode of producing and defining value. It is useful to extend this and reflect on perspectives that are emerging for new developments – and this means of course as well – as matter of a critique of political economy not least for countries in Latin America – here presented again in Overview 7.

Asia	EUrope	Latin America?/World?
MODE OF SOCIETAL PRODUCTION		
Large scale industrial production according to Fordist rules, and adapting post-Fordist techniques Adapting Fordist patterns as well in the area of IT-industries Maintained family business structures – literally but as well in terms of management methods – securing integration via collectivist-paternalist systems	Post-Fordist with an increasing number of small enterprises with a semi-independent status Dominant niche production and high-end refining on large production scales Increasingly searching for new methods of governance in politics and economics in order to establish more open structures, reflecting the demeaning of territorialism	Open project work, oriented on and social sustaina-responsibility and maintained by a basic income for all, thus the socio-economic conditions being secured The obligation on social sustaina-responsibility securing social recognition
MODE OF SOCIETALLY CONSTITUTING DISTRIBUTION		
To large extent family oriented and clientelist systems (this can mean as well orientation along different lines of community led services) Supporting somewhat community-based integration	Highly institutionally-contributory systems, linked into 'market solidarities' Subsequently individualist understanding of social provision	Both, subsistence and publicly secured securitisation for all, guaranteeing social inclusion
MODE OF PRODUCING AND DEFINING VALUE		
Production and refining oriented, this includes including service delivery into this chain	Highly financial market driven, gaining a partial and temporary independences from immediate production spheres	The immediate requirement of social sustaina-responsibility aiming on the establishment of cooperative structures, securing empowerment

Overview 7. Production, Distribution and Values.

It is important to highlight, another time, that there is no automatism between economic (=GDP-)growth and wealth or/and improvement of living conditions. A Communication from the Commission of the European Communities manifested the paradox – though surely not being aware of it. We read that '[m]ore recently, a study by the World Bank* shows that the opening of markets and economic integration have also contributed to substantial economic progress for developing countries that have managed to enter global manufacture and service markets. In the latest wave of globalisation, countries such as China, India and Mexico have doubled their ratio of trade to income, with their exports being made up increasingly of finished products and services, not just raw materials**. Such countries have on average increased their annual per capita economic growth from 1% in the 1960s to 3% in the 1970s and 5% in the 1990s. With such growth rates, often above those of OECD countries, these developing countries are now showing signs of convergence.' *(Commission of the European Communities, 2004: 4; with references: * Globalization, Growth and Poverty, 2002. **In India, for example, IT exports now account for nearly 40% of export earnings)*

However, that it is a convergence towards a structurally crisis-shaken world is not considered. Of course it would be shortsighted and could be called social-romanticism to seek for a development of an autarkic, no-growth development.[11] This means the other way round that both, GDP-growth and external trade have to play important roles. However, importantly trade balances are not simply quantitative relationships. As much as a balance, solely based on export of raw-materials, is highly problematic, the 'sweat-shop'-development of many industries – even if it is 'sweat-shops' in service industries – is highly problematic. Also, though export is important, the export-excess of many OECD-countries and in particular the 'strong countries' show exactly the problem of such convergence. These are economies that managed exorbitant short-term growth (as Ireland, the former exemplary student of the EU) and/or these are economies of which the working-class and their representatives are under immense pressure – we should not forget the austerity politics for instance in Germany and The Netherlands;[12] nor should we forget the 'agreements' which had been made for instance in parts of the German (state-controlled) car-manufacturing sector (VW) where workers had been confronted with the 'alternative' of agreeing to wage-cuts and unpaid reduction of working hours versus job-losses (the sometimes so-called 'Brazilianisation' in the OECD-countries). In addition to the failure of 'growth-only-assumption' and the matter of trade-balance which has to be taken in more differentiated ways *(see also Memedovic/Iapadre, 2009; UNCTAD, without date [2012]),* we have to address another aspect when we search new strategies: cooperatives as well as open project work are forms that will have to be reconsidered. The first is obviously a well-known framework – being rooted in various strands of the working class movement *(see in this context for instance Piñeiro Harnecker [comp.], 2012);* the other may be carefully reconsidered, asking if Schumpeterian entrepreneurs may actually take the form of immediately socialised forms of entrepreneurship – both, the questions of social security and social sustaina-responsibility posed as being of utmost importance.

Ad 4

All this means in particular re-establishing the true metabolism that is entailed in production proper. The most-far reaching separation characterising the development of the productive forces is actually the one that is concerned with the tendency of overcoming the dependency of or at least stretching the distance between human kind and nature. It is not about rejecting rationalisation and a rebuke of technical progress. However, it is about

[11] The debate on 'commons' and also 'de-growth' strategies can surely give important impulses but they have to be taken with care, considering their limitations nit least given by the conditions from which they emerge.

[12] The latter deserves special mention as the Dutch King recently announced the end of the welfare state http://www.independent.co.uk/news/world/europe/dutch-king-willemalexander-declares-the-end-of-the-welfare-state-8822421.html - 25/10/2013

rejecting a dominance of technisation that leads to a stage where we are producing without knowing the reason behind it.

I want to conclude with a remark taken from speech given by Ernesto Che Guervara, addressing his co-workers at the ministry of industry in 1961, facing new challenges:

> We can all contribute with our own efforts, everybody with his/her own view which may be very different; and based on his/her own convictions which may also be very different, but always aiming on contributing in the vital work – leaving the figures behind, as far as this is possible, interpreting the reality as it really is. That does not mean to return to the short-sighted practicism of the first days but we have to find a point of reference to combine the two essential things in an optimal way: namely on the one hand the practical and immediate knowledge, the reality and communication amongst us and on the other side the large abstract effort which is necessary to fulfil our tasks. (Guevara, October 6th, 1961: 63 – translation P.H.)

References

Blair, Hugh, 1787: *Lectures on rhetoric and belles lettres*; in: Birindellei, Massimo (1981): Piazza San Pietro; Roma/Bari: Editori Laterza.

Boccara, Paul, 2010: La crise systémique: une crise de civilisation. Ses perspectives pour avancer vers une nouvelle civilisation, note de la Fondation Gabriel Péri.

Bosniak, Linda, 2000: Citizenship Denationalized; in: *Indiana Journal of Global Legal Studies,* 7: 447-509.

Commission of the European Communities, 2004: The Social Dimension of Globalisation – the EU's policy contribution on extending the benefits to all. Communication from the Commission to the European Parliament, the Council, the European Economic and Social Committee and the Committee of the Regions; Brussels, 18.5.2004 COM(2004) 383 final.

Engels, Frederick, 1884: The Origin of the Family, Private Property and the State [in the light of the researches by Lewis H. Morgan]; in: Karl Marx. Frederick Engels. *Collected Works*. Volume 26. Engels: 1882-1889; London: Laurence&Wishart, 1990: 129-276.

Galbraith, J.K. 1976: The Affluent Society. Boston: Houghton Mifflin.

Globalization, *Growth and Poverty – A World Bank Policy Research Report*, World Bank and Oxford University Press, 2002.

Gore, Charles, 1996: Methodological Nationalism and the Misunderstanding of East Asian Industrialisation; in: *European Journal of Development Research;* 8, 77-122 [1 June 1996]: 80 doi: 10.1080/09578819608426654.

Guevara, Ernesto Che, October 6th, 1961: Gibt es ein Recht auf Verschwendung; in: Che Guevara, Ernesto: Der Neue Mensch. Entwürfe für das Leben in der Zukunft. Selected, interpreted and introduced by Horst-Eckart Gross; Dortmund: Weltkreis: 1984: 61-80.

Heath, Joseph, 2000: Should Productivity Growth Be a Social Priority?; in: *The Review of Economic Performance and Social Progress*: 227-241; here: 231.

Herrmann, Peter, 2010: Globalization Revisited; in: Society and Economy 32 [2010] 2: 255–275; here: 268; DOI: 10.1556/SocEc.32.2010.2.6.

Herrmann, Peter, 2013: Human Rights – Good Will Hunting vs. Taking Positions; in: Kalaycioglu, Sibel/Herrmann, Peter [eds.], 2013: *Social Policy and Religion*; New York: Nova.

Hirsch, J., 2005: *Materialistische Staatstheorie*; Hamburg: VSA.

Ivorra, Pierre, 2013: Crise de civilisation, crise de 2008-2010 et solutions systémiques; in: Économie&Politique. Revue marxiste d'économie; 708-709, Juillet-Août 2013; 39-39.

Lorenz, E. and Lundvall, B.Å. (2011): 'Accounting for Creativity in the European Union: A multi-level analysis of individual competence, labour market structure, and systems of life-long learning', Cambridge Journal of Economics Vol 35 No. 2 pp. 269-294.

Marx, Karl, 1843/44: Contribution to the Critique of Hegel's Philosophy of Law. Introduction; in: Karl Marx. Frederick Engels. Collected Works. Volume 3: Marx and Engels 1843-1844; London: Lawrence & Wishart, 1975: 175-187.

Marx, Karl, 1844: Economic and Philosophical Manuscripts; in: Karl Marx Frederick Engels. *Collected Works Volume 3: Marx and Engels 1843-1844*; London: Laurence&Wishart, 1975: 229-346.

Marx, Karl, 1867: Capital Vol. I; in: *Karl Marx. Frederick Engels. Collected Works;* Volume 35; London: Lawrence&Wishart, 1996.

Memedovic, Olga/Iapadre, Lelio, 2009: Structural Change in the World Economy: Main Features and Trends; Working Paper 24/2009; Vienna: UNIDO, 2010.

Perez, Carlota, 2012: Innovation systems and policies: not only for the rich?; Working Papers in *Technology Governance and Economic Dyananmics* no. 42; Norway: The Other Canon Foundation/Tallinn: Tallinn University of Technology.

Piñeiro Harnecker, Camila [comp.], 2012: Cooperativas y Socialismo. Una Mirada desde Cuba; La Habana: Editorial Caminos.

Poulantzas, Nicco, 1978: *State, Power*, Socialism; London: Verso.

Roche, Maurice, 1992: *Rethinking Citizenship: Welfare, Ideology, and Change in Modern Society*; Polity: 184 f.

Rupp, Hans Heinrich, 1991: Grundfragen der heutigen Verwaltungsrechtslehre; Tübingen: Mohr Siebeck.

Schmalz, Stefan/Ebenau, Matthias, 2012: After Neoliberalism? Brazil, India, and China in the Global Economic Crisis; in: Globalizations, August 2012, Vol. 9, No. 4, pp. 487–501, here: 490

Sousa Santos, Boaventura de, 1997: Hacia una concepción multicultural de los derechos humanos: 15; http://democraciayterritorio.wordpress.com/2008/08/09/hacia-una-concepcion-multicultural-de-los-derechos-humanos/ - 06/10/13.

Steinberg, Philip E., 2009: Sovereignty, Territory, and the Mapping of Mobility: A View from the Outside; in: *Annals of the Association of American Geographers*; 99, 3, 467-495.

UNCTAD, without date [2012]: Investment Policy Framework for Sustainable Development; http://unctad.org/en/PublicationsLibrary/webdiaepcb2012d6_en.pdf - 25/10/2013.

van der Maesen, Laurent J.G., November 20th, 2012: Working-paper no 9: Elaboration of a Lecture on the Orientation, Strategies and Model (or Experiences) of the City of Hangzhou (Zhejiang province of mainland China), from a comparative; working papers at http://socialquality.eu/ - 20/09/2013.

van der Maesen, Laurent J.G./Walker, Alan, 2012: *Social Quality and Sustainability*; in: Van der Maesen, Laurent J.G./Walker, Alan (eds.): *Social Quality. From Theory to Indicators*: Basingstoke: Palgrave Macmillan; 250-274.

Vogl, Joseph (2010): *Das Gespenst des Kapitals;* Zürich.

Part I. Scene XIX: Night
(The Street in front of Gretchen's door)

Mephistopheles:
Now, the lout is tamed!
Away, we must go! Swiftly, of course
(219)

http://images-02.delcampe-static.net/img_large/auction/000/163/584/385_007.jpg - 04.01.15

Chapter 6

ENVIRONMENTAL DEMOCRACY – NEW CHALLENGES[1]

ABSTRACT

Environmental Democracy itself is a topic that is of more or less recent origin, demanding measures in the framework of environmental protection (though in a wide sense) as matter that includes democratic processes. Of course, this changes the character of democracy itself. But the relevance of another link is barely considered: the issue of life style. The thesis presented in the following is grounded in four core points:

- the question of environmental sustainability is increasingly a question of changing the way in which we produce and reproduce our social relationships – making reference to the social quality approach is a valuable cornerstone
- the change is very much also a reflection of objective changes of the mode of production – political economy has to gain acknowledgement within the social quality framework
- a major challenge is about a change of understanding democracy – considerations will be taken from theories of deliberative and participatory democracy
- finally the understanding of 'environment' will be considered – reflections will be inspired by a reinterpretation of sociological systems theory, economics (questions of productive forces and means of production) and anthropological studies (the understanding of 'nature' as predominant point of reference).

The presentation will conclude with reflections on the practical consequences for local, regional and global policy-making.

[1] Presentation for the International Conference of Environmental Democracy and Social Quality; Hangzhou; June 2014. I have to apologise that there is in large parts an overtly dominance of Western thinking that determines part of the text and thoughts.

INTRODUCTION

Imagination is more important than knowledge. For knowledge is limited, whereas imagination embraces the entire world, stimulating progress, giving birth to evolution. It is, strictly speaking, a real factor in scientific research. (Einstein)

One of the ongoing problems of discussing sustainability is the lack of a clear definition. The actual problem is not the lack of such definition itself but the claim that we need such description. Einstein supposedly said 'the environment is everything that isn't me'. Such open definition invites to imagination and accepting the fact of the multiple dimensions environment and environmental issues have. At least the following are seen as essential for the present context, namely the discussion of environmental democracy:

- it is a matter of the organic nature
- it is concerned with the inorganic, i.e., human-made surrounding
- it is about the people around us, and with this a matter of the social itself
- and not least it is about how we as human beings relate to this environment.

Furthermore, it is important to emphasise at the outset the necessity of distinguishing between the environment itself and environmental issues, understood as perception of and dealing with issues that concern the environment. However, crucially important is the fundamental and widening process of disembedding and dichotomisation. For the current subject, the following are the most decisive dimensions:[2]

- the constitution of human existence as centre, thus establishing (and following) the rule from the biblical order defined in Genesis 1/28 which states: 'fill the earth and subdue it' (the roots being Christianity and capitalism)
- the subsequent separation of human beings and human existence from nature (the roots being Christian and Cartesian thinking)
- the juxtaposing of individuals and society (the roots being Western enlightenment and the [in part] subsequent utilitarianism)
- and finally the dissolution of the economy and economic processes from the wider social and societal processes (analysed by Karl Polanyi).

When taking this as reference, we have can see some fundamental shortcomings of the concept of environmental democracy. Such critique will be based in a very short presentation of the main lines of the understanding as they are defined by the Summit in Rio and the Aarhus Declaration.

Against this background the understanding of some basic principles and concepts will be outlined, especially aiming on developing the social quality approach further by highlighting the aspect of production and reproduction of everyday's life. Finally, by way of conclusion, this will allow some policy recommendations as challenge of mainstream thinking, but also in order to develop social quality thinking further. Sure, at the end we still face the question of

[2] See for the following also the inspiring text by *Moore, 2014 a, b)*

defining sustainability in the light of social quality thinking, not least by asking for democracy in the era of socio-ecological citizenship.

ENVIRONMENTAL DEMOCRACY

Environmental democracy is a neologism that was already a torso when it entered the agenda. The reason is simple, consisting of the connection between the following factors:

- both core terms, environment and democracy, are ill-defined
- their combination makes actually a definition of each of them even more difficult
- nevertheless, the environmental problems and their increasing severity are undeniable, and also the perception of these problems, some of them existing in fact already for centuries, is increasing
- and finally any solution is confronted with the challenge of legitimacy not least in the light of fundamental changes that are standing at the end of any attempt dealing with the environmental issues.

A highly simplified answer is given by the *Convention on Access to Information, Public Participation in Decision-Making and Access to Justice in Environmental Matters* done at Aarhus, Denmark, on 25 June 1998 *(Convention, 1998)*. At the core there are three pillars outlined in the title, namely 'Access to Environmental Information' *(article 4)*, 'Public Participation in Decisions on Specific Activities' *(article 6)* and 'Access to Justice' *(article 9)*. These three pillars are complemented by two decisive structural moments. The first is the underlying definition of environment. As the reference of the convention is the Rio Declaration from 1992, the core principle has to be seen in the claim that '[h]uman beings are at the centre of concerns for sustainable development. They are entitled to a healthy and productive life in harmony with nature.' *(United Nations, 1992)*

This, of course, maintains an anthropocentric worldview.

The second important issue is that the principle of democracy is limited, one point being the lack of opportunities to decide about the actual relevance. In other words, the substantive rights are widely limited whereas the procedural rights are emphasised.

A CRITICAL REPROACH

Some critical points are already mentioned, immediately in connection with the presentation of the concept. The following have to be seen as fundamental:

Anthropocentrism defines a principal limitation to the question of environmental democracy. It does not allow to fundamentally question the supposed superiority of human beings, which means in turn that the utilitarian approach towards the environment is set in stone as long as this anthropocentrism is not overcome. This means the other way round that we have to emphasise another time the fact: The environmental crisis is in actual fact a socio-anthropological crisis.

However, we have to be careful, as this anthropological crisis is not simply about humankind as such – understood as a homogenous agency. Instead, anthropocentrism veils the fact that we are dealing with a historically specific relationship not only between humankind and 'external nature'. In other words, truly important is the relationship between human beings and the historically given understanding of what 'good life' and 'good society' is about. In other words, we are dealing with an understanding that fosters an instrumental understanding of resources: understanding human grandeur as being limitless, means that the subordinated environment has to serve this strive to unlimited growth.

In consequence a utilitarian approach to both, environment and democracy is maintained: the environment needs to be protected but is itself not considered to be part of a co-productive setting. In other words, this approach maintains the dualist structure that sees relevant issues as environmental problems, not as problems of humans, humanity and their (mis-)behaviour. In this contribution only a short hint can be presented: according to Earthjustice 'Numerous constitutions of the nations of the world guarantee a right to a clean and healthy environment or a related right. Of the approximately 193 countries of the world, there are now 117 whose national constitutions mention the protection of the environment or natural resources.' *(Earthjustice, 2005: 37).* – This stands not least in connection with an instrumentalist interpretation of the environment:

> At the beginning of this third millennium, there should be no doubt that human activities can cause serious environmental problems, or that those problems, in turn, often result in grave harm to human beings. Put positively, a clean and healthy environment is essential to the realization of fundamental human rights. (ibid.: 1)

However, though a thorough analysis remains to be undertaken, it is well known that the *right of nature* remains by and large limited to few cases, being especially some Latin American countries. Without denying the importance of protective measures, the limitation should be clear: the approach is geared to damage control, leaving by and large a more fundamental questioning of the mode of production and the related living regimes out of consideration. Consequently, Jason W. Moore criticises rightly 'an ontological agreement: the 'co-production of society WITH nature', as if these were two independent entities. While co-production is the right way to put it, its association with a Nature/Society vocabulary short-circuits the effort to move from modernity WITH nature towards modernity-in-nature.' *(Moore,2014 (a): 6 – see for detailed references the original text)*

With this consideration in mind, it is remarkable that – especially when it comes to internationally relevant political documents – only very few definitions refer to the environment in a wider sense, for instance the *International Court of Justice* contending that it 'also recognizes that the environment is not an abstraction but represents the living space, the quality of life and the very health of human beings, including generations unborn.' *(International Court of Justice, 1996)*

Consolidating Social Quality Thinking

It is somewhat easy – and surely necessary – to criticise the current economic system for being negligibly considering the environmental costs of a one sided growth orientation –

although such interpretation may surely start from many different viewpoints. It is surely also easy – and perhaps even more so – to blame individuals' greediness. And finally it is of course relative easy, necessary and still also misleading to emphasise the neglect of immaterial values by the current economic growth dynamic and the subsequent utilitarian orientation. Brand and Wissen contend that

> [t]he important point for our argument is the assumption that in certain historical phases, and building on a coherence between norms of production and of consumption, a hegemonic – or in other words – broadly accepted and institutionally secured mode of living can emerge that is deeply rooted in the everyday practices of people and safeguarded by the state, and it is further associated with certain concepts of progress: computers must be ever more powerful and food ever cheaper – regardless of the social or ecological conditions under which they are produced. (Brand/Wissen, 2012: 549)

However, this position remains hugely problematic as it does not sufficiently address the underlying mechanisms.

In the following two strands will be drawn together, the first is concerned with political economy, the second a definition of sustainability in the light of social quality will be approached.

I.[3]

An initial point of reference can be seen in the work of Kondratieff and the bol'shie tsiklys, i.e., major cycles and the respective discussion that followed his proposals. The aim of the specific interpretation I want to suggest is twofold. With this reference we can determine major shifts of the current modes of production and their objective dimension. As such it also allows pushing the social quality thinking further, working on the meaning of the structure, structuration and change of political economy (as reality of the political economy and the analysis alike). Instead of simply referring to the broad changes, Kondratieff claimed himself that his approach would be by and large descriptive, not aiming on providing an analysis in the strict sense – it is necessary to draw on other paradigms – the reason for this can be found in the definition of the social itself, which is seen as 'an outcome of the interaction between people (constituted as actors) and their constructed and natural environment. Its subject matter refers to people's interrelated productive and reproductive relationships.' *(van der Maesen, Laurent J.G./Walker, Alan, 2012: 260)*

For developing a sound understanding of these productive and reproductive relationships it is fruitful to interpret the approach to major cycles with help of a systematic combination of the following approaches and paradigms:

- an extended understanding of the French theory of regulation, looking at the accumulation regime and mode of regulation, and using this for an exploration of specific living regimes and modes of life – part of this has to take the debate on the varieties of capitalism into account though those debates are in two ways

[3] The following section had been already presented in a very similar way in *Herrmann, Peter, 2014; see also in this volume the contribution on* Social Quality – Social Anomie. Two Sides of one Coin?

reductionist: (a) they are commonly only concerned with the micro level and (b) the proposed degree of variation is in fact extremely limited

- World Systems Theory, allowing to recognise the social division of labour on a global level, but going beyond this by suggesting the 'accommodation of different modes of production within the one capitalist system' *(see also page 56 f.)*
- the distinction and drawing together of the different moments of the process of production, namely production in the strict sense, consumption, distribution and exchange – this can be seen as matter of accumulation regime and living regime
- and not least the reference to Karl Polanyi, who importantly distinguishes between reciprocity, distribution and market as mechanisms of steering; not less important is his discussion of embeddedness of economic activities – this can be seen as matter of mode of regulation and mode of life.

II.

In the perspective of social quality thinking two major challenges of today's societies and societal developments are individualism and utilitarism as principles and driving forces of structuration. These are not 'unwelcome' normative strives, but mechanism characterising the social as it is defined as interplay of conditional, constitutional and normative factors along two tensional lines: the one between communities and institutions and the other between biographical and societal development.[4]

This means that we have to look for a definition of sustainability that fulfils two criteria: first it has to go beyond the commonly used reference to environment as by and large *undefined externality* that is in need of protection; second, we have to make sure that the aspect of co-production between social human beings and the environment is reflected in the definition of sustainability. The second point had been already presented in the previous section – it is important to keep this in mind when it comes to developing concrete policies. An earlier definition of sustainability had been given, seeing it as

> 'a state of dynamic equilibrium between the entire interactive ensemble of non-living and living entities, functioning within the boundaries of a resilient system'. These living entities include the complexities of human actions. These complexities can cause either sustainable or unsustainable societal relationships as well as sustainable or unsustainable conditions concerning the resilience boundaries.
>
> (van Renswoude, Jos/van der Meaesen, Laurent J.G. van der Maesen, 2012: 3)

In the following I will try to establish an explicit and thus closer link to the social quality architecture, having in mind environmental democracy as a point of reference that only evolved in this context recently.

[4] For the architecture of the social quality approach see the various contributions in *van der Maesen, Laurent J.G./Walker, Alan (eds.), 2012)*.

- Rights are not bound to agency in the sense of individual actors but seen as matter of entities that are constitutive part of the social – this means that rights are granted to 'the interaction between people (constituted as actors) and their constructed and natural environment'[5]: both, interaction, people and the environment itself are bearers of rights. – This concerns mainly the *tension between communities and institutions.*
- 'Identifiable interest', legitimately constitutive for defining and granting rights, are not self-referential; instead, they are defined by the relationality which reflects the definition of the social, speaking of 'people's interrelated productive and reproductive relationships'.[6] – This concerns mainly the *tension between biographical and societal development.*
- Rights and obligations have to be discussed in this light and responsibility as an additional dimension has to be looked at, especially dealing with the *normative factors* of the architecture.
- Rights (and obligations) also need to be discussed again in the light of the *conditional factors,* which themselves have to be defined (or redefined) by way of the relational dimension of (re-)production. This allows not least emphasising the productive dimension of both, human beings, humanity and the environment.
- Finally it is necessary to look at the productive forces and elaborate a new take on this point by emphasising relationality. With some justification this can be seen as matter of material and non-material growth. However, the limit of the justification is given by (i) maintaining the centrality of growth and (ii) the subsequent lack of questioning the character of production. This is especially a matter of the *constitutional factors.*

In short, environmental democracy in the context of social quality thinking requires first highlighting the fact that the environment is co-actor within the processuality of the production of the social – the definition of the social already points into this direction, speaking of 'the interaction between people (constituted as actors) and their constructed and natural environment'. However it requires, second, acknowledging the right of the environment which implies to see the environment also as active part of the interaction. Third, it means that the question of growth is not about juxtaposing material and non-material growth. Instead, the question is not even concerned with the quality of growth. Instead it has to be centred on the quality of production. This leads finally to the orientation on the most fundamental question: the 're-embedding' of production into the entirety of social and societal relationships.

[5] Taken from the definition presented earlier
[6] Taken from the definition presented earlier

CONCLUSIONS – FURTHERING THE WAY TO SUSTAINABLE URBAN DEVELOPMENT

Though this is first and foremost highly theoretical, it is relevant when it comes to concrete matters of policy making. We can start for instance with the reference to the *Leipzig Charter on Sustainable European Cities,* brought forward in 2007 under the German EU-presidency. It speaks about strengthening local economies and importantly it also mentions the need 'to create better conditions and instruments to strengthen the local economy and thus the local labour markets, in particular by promoting the social economy and providing citizen-friendly services.' *(Leipzig Charter, 2007: 6).*

In other words, it encourages also the change of the productive process in the sense of societal praxis. It should be added that the concept of commons requires to be revisited and utilised for further development. This highlights another problem that is widely discussed: the issue of decoupling. The main orientation is usually seeing the technical dimension of the given constellation – in the following for instance presented by the UNEP.

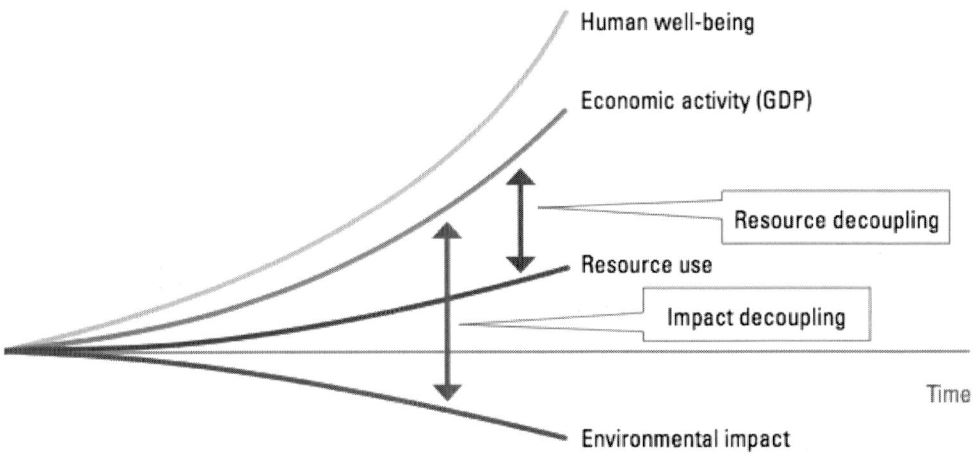

(UNEP, 2011: XIII).

Figure 1. Two Aspects of Decoupling.

However, this neglects completely the main problematique, namely the underlying fact that economic activities, resource use and environmental impact are seen in isolation, leaving the human well-being outside of the consideration. In other words, it does not look at the disembedded economy itself – the economy, we may term provocatively, is seen as a- or non-social issue. Governance – and this is also the major challenge in terms of environmental democracy – is not simply about changing the pattern of the increasing distance between city and society *(see Beguinot et al., 2011; quoted in: van der Maesen, assisted by Peter Herrmann, 2012: 8).* More important is the distance between the social and the economy and the separation of politics from both. Further discussions are needed, not least striving for a clear and operational understanding of socio-ecological citizenship which has to be developed as core of environmental democracy. We may start from the following:

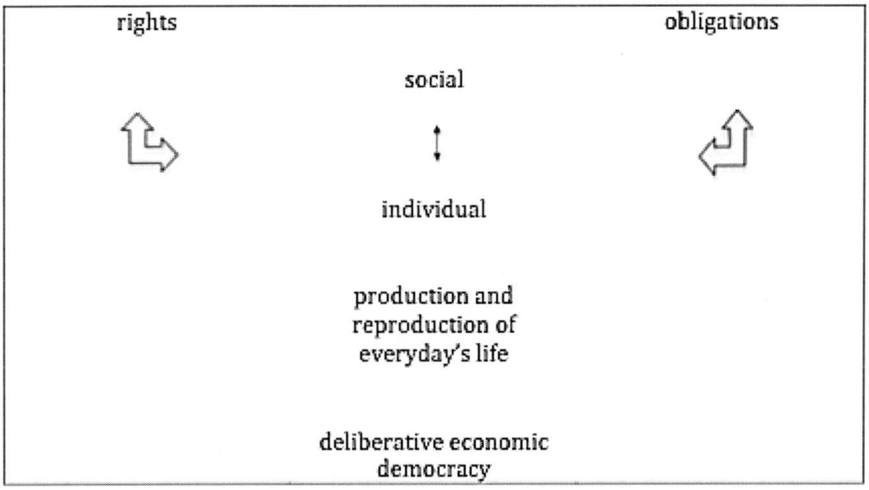

Figure 8. Socio-Ecological Citizenship.

Some general points have to be addressed – here only mentioned as questions.[7] The first is concerned with the well-known common limitation of citizenship, founded in the ongoing reference to the (nation) state. Ecological problems are mainly global and also local. This requires to look for ways of strengthening the local dimension, however at the same time firmly linking this to the global dimension of globality. As much as the nation-state served as point of reference for defining a common good, this may have to be replaced by socio-ecological sustainability.

A second and systematically linked aspect is concerned with the relationship of public and private which cannot be maintained as such. As much as oikonomia emerged beyond its original border of a household economy,[8] its private character cannot be maintained. This means not least that the concept of private, for profit business needs as well to be transformed and adapted to some fundamental mechanisms of socialisation *(see in this context for instance Sukhdev).*

Furthermore this requires emphasising the importance of deliberative democracy that intrinsically links aspects of 'local communities' with the dimension of the mode of regulation. With this link, it can be possible to overcome NIMBY-orientations and also the hegemony of one-dimensional global alliances.

Immediate Challenges Ahead

In a very final step of the current contribution, I want to pose four major tools or mechanisms that may be applied for pushing the relevant debates on socio-environmental sustainability forward (i) and four major challenges that have to be seen as major potential threats or hindrances (ii).

[7] see for further discussion: *Dobson/Bell, 2006; Dobson, 2007*

[8] as such it had been considered as 'private affair'

(i) Pushing debates on socio-environmental sustainability forward

- *Citizenship Education* – it is surely only a mechanism that can work in a very long term perspective, at the same time it can be used as instrument that possibly leads to a long term change of attitudes, especially if teaching takes place by way of 'practice teaching', i.e., developing the awareness in connection with active involvement of pupils into processes of policy making.
- *'Citizenry of Communities' instead of Service Orientation* – it can be developed and applied in different ways and different settings – reaching from schools, civil society organisations, and statutory organisations. The crucial point is to develop an understanding and reality of co-ownership that goes beyond lip services, allowing real control.
- *Participative Budgeting* – this can be a major step when it comes to decision-making, not least allowing establishing an immediate link between executing political influence and part of the economic dimension, it also allows establishing an immediate link between economic policies and every day's life.
- *Public Transport and Use of Space as Part of Commons* – both, the development of Citizenry and (in connection with) Participative Budgeting can be considered as moments that allow the development of commons. Linking public transport and use of space in this context, may enforce linking in very concrete terms local and global issues.

(ii) Potential Threats and Hindrances on the Way Forward

- *'Modesty'* – an ongoing and anthropological[9] challenge is that of 'recognising sufficiency' which is also a matter of accepting borders and limits.
- *Changing Attitudes and Behaviour* – leaving the dominance of the objective forces aside, the challenge remains to address attitudes (and behaviour). Actually the before-mentioned aspect of developing citizenry as matter of participatory deliberation can serve as tool, developing attitudes from the outset as constitutive for individuals acting consciously as social beings.
- *'Limits to Self-Limitation' (e.g., working conditions, 'luxury')* – one point should never be forgotten: considering mechanisms and attitudes that are concerned with self-limitation and modesty while living on a level of high standards, is one thing; however, there are two other perspectives. The one is about a still existing need to strive for even the minimum of provisions. In several cases this is actually depending on sustainability – we may think about the right to (access to) water for all, being undermined by private control, the latter undermining sustainable development. In other cases this is however not the case: provision of the minimum often requires expansion of production, meaning increased energy use, exploitation of raw materials etc. . The other point is about asking if and when limitations are reasonable – a very

[9] To be sure, anthropological has here as always be seen in its historical context, not being matter of humankind in general.

crude example is the use of mechanical tools for heavy labour versus applying easy-to-use machines which consume energy, cause emission etc.. Another example is concerned with mobility, i.e., the questions *How mobile should we be?* and *Which means should we use?*

- *Equality, Justice and Enforceability* – though we will easily find a general agreement on the validity of equality and justice as universal values, we will surely find it difficult to define such values in concrete terms. An additional moment has to look at the question if such general values, if agreed by the majority, should be enforced – the old Rousseauean question of relating the will of all with the general will.

These are serious and very practical questions. It would be presumptuous to say that the social quality approach can easily give answers. But based on the experience gathered during the projects on urban development, it is promising to consider social quality offering a useful methodology that allows finding relevant answers. It allows a systemic approach that does not solely and primarily look at the processes of production. It goes further by also asking for recognition of the social and natural embeddness of this process.

REFERENCES

Beck, W./van der Maesen, L. J. G./Walker, A., 2012. Theoretical Foundations. In: van der Maesen, L.J.G/A. Walker (eds.), 2012: *Social Quality: From Theory to Indicators.* Basingstoke: Palgrave Macmillan: 44–69.

Beguinot, C. et al, 2011: The City Crises: For a UN World Conference and for a UN Resolution. *The Priority of the XX1 Century*; Napoli: Giannini, 323 Eighth Tome Series of Urban Studies.

Brand, Ulrich/Wissen, Markus, 2012: Global Environmental Politics and the Imperial Mode of Living: Articulations of State–Capital Relations in the Multiple Crisis; in: *Globalizations,* 9:4, 547-560; http://dx.doi.org/10.1080/14747731.2012.699928).

Convention on Access to Information, Public Participation in Decision-Making and Access to Justice in Environmental Matters done at Aarhus, Denmark, on 25 June 1998 (http://www.unece.org/env/pp/treatytext.html; English version at http://www.unece.org/fileadmin/DAM/env/pp/documents/cep43e.pdf; 15/06/2014.

Dobson, Andrew, 2007: Environmental Citizenship: Towards Sustainable Development; in: *Sustainable Development.* Sust. Dev. 15, 276–285 (2007); Published online in Wiley InterScience (www.interscience.wiley.com) DOI: 10.1002/sd.344.

Dobson, Andrew/Bell, Derek, 2006: Introduction; in: Dobson, Andrew/Bell, Derek (eds.): Environmental Citizenship; Cambridge, Massachusetts/London, England: The MIT Press.

Earthjustice, 2005: Environmental Rights Report. Human Rights and the Environment; Materials for the 61st Session of the United Nations Commission on Human Rights. Geneva, March 14 – April 22; Oakland 2005.

Einstein, Albert: Cosmic Religion: With Other Opinions and Aphorisms (1931) by Albert Einstein, p. 97; also in Transformation: Arts, Communication, Environment (1950) by Harry Holtzman, p. 138; http://en.wikiquote.org/wiki/Albert_Einstein; 15/06/2014.

Herrmann, Peter, 2014: Social Quality – Social Anomie. Two Sides of one Coin?; Notes made in preparation of a presentation of the Hungarian Academy of Science, June 12th, 2014 – preliminary paper which will be elaborated.

International Court of Justice. Reports of Judgments, Advisory Opinions and Orders: Legality of the Threat or Use of Nuclear Weapons. Advisory Opinion of 8 July 1996; http://www.icj-cij.org/docket/files/95/7495.pdf; 15/06/2014.

Leipzig Charter on Sustainable European Cities: 6 - http://ec.europa.eu/regional_policy/archive/themes/urban/leipzig_charter.pdf - 16/06/2014.

Moore, Jason W., March 2014 (a): The Capitalocene. Part I: On the Nature & Origins of Our Ecological Crisis; March 2014 (http://www.jasonwmoore.com/uploads/The_Capitalocene__Part_I__June_2014.pdf - 15/06/2014.

Moore, Jason W., March 2014 (b): The Capitalocene. Part II: Abstract Social Nature and the Limits to Capital; March 2014, Minor revisions June 2014 (http://www.jasonwmoore.com/uploads/The_Capitalocene___Part_II__June_2014.pdf - 15/06/2014.

Moore, Jason W., March 2014: The Capitalocene. Part I: On the Nature & Origins of Our Ecological Crisis; March 2014: 6 [http://www.jasonwmoore.com/uploads/The_Capitalocene__Part_I__June_2014.pdf - 15/06/2014.

Sukhdev, Pavan, Corporation 2020. Transforming Business for Tomorrows World; Washington: Island Press.

UNEP, 2011: Decoupling natural resource use and environmental impacts from economic growth, A Report of the Working. Group on Decoupling to the International Resource Panel. Fischer-Kowalski, M., Swilling, M., von Weizsäcker, E.U., Ren, Y.,Moriguchi, Y., Crane, W., Krausmann, F., Eisenmenger, N., Giljum, S., Hennicke, P., Romero Lankao, P., Siriban Manalang, A., Sewerin, S.; http://www.unep.org/resourcepanel/decoupling/files/pdf/decoupling_report_english.pdf - 15/06/2014.

United Nations, General Assembly, August 12th, 1992: Rio Declaration on Environment and Development; Principle 1; http://www.un.org/documents/ga/conf151/aconf15126-1annex1.htm; 15/06/2014.

van der Maesen Laurent J.G., assisted by Peter Herrmann, 2012: Welfare Arrangements, Sustainable Urban Development, and New forms of Governance: the current 'demonstration project' of the City of The Hague as example Plans for the start of comparative urban studies between The Hague, Sheffield and Hangzhou as point of departure for the European GOSUD-project; Draft Working-paper nr.8.

van der Maesen, Laurent J.G., November 20th, 2012: Working-paper no 9: Elaboration of a Lecture on the Orientation, Strategies and Model [or Experiences] of the City of Hangzhou [Zhejiang province of mainland China], from a comparative; working papers at http://socialquality.eu/ - 20/09/2013.

van der Maesen, Laurent J.G./Walker, Alan (eds.), 2012: *Social Quality*. From Theory to Indicators: Basingstoke: Palgrave Macmillan.

van der Maesen, Laurent J.G./Walker, Alan, 2012: *Social Quality and Sustainability*; in: van der Maesen, Laurent J.G./Walker, Alan (eds.): *Social Quality. From Theory to Indicators*: Basingstoke: Palgrave Macmillan; 250-274.

van Renswoude, Jos/van der Meaesen, Laurent J.G. van der Maesen, 2012: Development toward sustainability. *The need for a Comprehensive Conceptual and Methodological Framework for new politics and policies: A social quality perspective.* A contribution to the Rio+20 Conference on the sustainability of human existence on Earth. A Report presented by the International Association on Social Quality; http://www.socialquality.org/wp-content/uploads/2014/10/WorkingPaper-11-2012.pdf - 06/01/15.

Scene Prologue in Heaven

Mephistopeles:
I like to hear the Old Man's words, from time to time, And take care, when Iím with him, not to spew.
It is very nice when such a great Gentleman,
Chats with the devil, in ways so human, too!
(21)

http://imgc.allpostersimages.com/images/P-473-488-90/15/1507/B83BD00Z/posters/eugene-delacroix-mephistopheles-prologue-in-the-sky-from-goethe-s-faust-1828.jpg - 04/01/15

Chapter 7

CRISIS AND NO END!?[1]

ABSTRACT

There is no end of the crisis in sight – this is also openly recognised by the apologists of the system. But in fact, the task is still not to interpret the world; instead, important is to develop a more detailed and radical analysis, then allowing moving towards changing structures that are underlying the current situation.

The present contribution investigates the crisis in this light. The recently published analysis of the World Bank is taken as occasion to show that a central problem is not the analysis of key benchmarks, but the discussion of main paradigms as growth, nationality, statehood and the like which are by and large still seen as unquestionable. The lack of fundamental criticism of some key concepts is going hand in hand with critical objections from the left. In any case a radical shift is needed when we aim at a proactive re-interpretation of the future instead of following a simple linear pathway.

THESES

1. The discussion of the current crisis remains trapped by the old tracks – and it is often just looking at the glass, asking if it is half-empty or half-full, at the end being oriented on re-establishing a status-quo ante. This is in many cases also true in those cases where critique claims to fundamentally reject the existing system. However, when talking about a structural crisis, the question must be whether the glass is actually completely broken. This means as well do move the debate on the crisis beyond analysing the dramatic consequences, in particular the 'social costs'. We

[1] For the inspiration for writing this section and helpful comments on a first draft, I am particularly grateful to Christoph Mayer. Also the many discussions with colleagues from the EUROMEMORANDUM group had been an important source. Especially the collaboration and friendship with Marica Frangakis, especially beginning in 2011 in Vienna and furthered especially during the Baron meeting in Mainz, 2012 are much appreciated. I wand to extend my thanks to James Galbraith and Victoria Panova and the extensive conversation during the 2014-Sorrento-meeting – or more honest to say the long nights that had been going with it. – The present version is a translated, extended and edited version of a text that had been originally written in German, and published on the website of attac.de; a revised English version will be published in Environment and Social Psychology, I/I, 2016

have to analyse the crisis of American hegemony and its accumulation regime, related living regimes and national and international regulatory mechanisms.

2. Then, the current challenge is to look at the crisis of the hegemonic system.[12] If this is seen as power of ideas, it should also be emphasised that the so-called neoliberalism reflects a one-sided interpretation of the objective conditions and not simply a voluntary statement of values of a self-proclaimed ruling-class. Though this may sound at first glance trivial, such emphasis is still important. Only if it is considered that and in which way these hegemonic strategies are actually reflecting objective conditions, it will be possible to elaborate sound counter-proposals, not geared towards the limits of growth and a new morality (or even the recovery of an old, supposedly better moral as it is frequently seen in ancient life and taken up in the Renaissance and Classicism). Instead, needed is a courageous utopia, based in the objectively given conditions of the productive forces and the real potential, and partly implicitly realised in the existing forms of socialisation.
3. The 'limits to growth' are not simply a matter of discussing the negative constellations; it is necessary to consider the wider context, allowing to understand the *limits to growth* in the context of the ongoing *limits to limitations* that are to a large extent directly and causally related. We are talking about increasing inequalities, which are much more extensive than shown in xyz mainstream and standard publications on inequalty: It is still the question of the (lack of) access to basic resources such as water, nutrition, housing, etc., all this increasingly a problem in all societies.
4. Finally, politics are always made for an uncertain future – risks should not result in paralysis nor lead to excessive adjustments.

Crisis or What? Proposal for a Long-Term, Structure - Oriented Assessment of the Crisis

Crisis analysis – even on the political left – leaves too often out of consideration that the current situation is not simply one in which economically strong countries stand against economically weak countries. We are facing the fundamental of class policies: those at the top standing against those at the bottom, a battle of class struggle from above simultaneously on the national and the international level. Another point has to be seen: with the intensification of the class struggle within the EU it is easily forgotten that this is part of a shift of the balance of power on the global geopolitical level: the shifts within the EU are part of the aspirations of establishing global domination within a new unipolar world-order. Though this may seem trivial, it nevertheless deserves special attention: only this way we can highlight another trivialisation which is dominating the media in particular in parts of European media: the presumed thesis that 'the Germans' are the global crisis winners.

Looking at capital, we actually see a rather diverse picture. One question is whether the entire ruling classes are really winners and what role the different 'margins' play – though there is a ruling class, this is by no means a homogenous block. Another important question is

[2] See for instance Mahnkopf, 2010

concerned with the different positions within this class – details are certainly of great importance when it comes to the assessment and the subsequent proposals for developing 'policies for the future.'[3]

Of course, even structural crises are nothing special, but actually the norm of capitalist development. It is easy to grasp by looking at one exemplary point: Overproduction/underconsumption crises are a fundamental and constitutional aspect of the process of capitalist realisation. On the one hand, capital is geared to minimise costs;[4] however, on the other hand, putting this orientation into practice means to undermine demand – the realisation of capital is facing restrictive conditions: the simple version of this constellation is the reduction of effective demand. However, we are currently experiencing a far more complex constellation, which will be briefly looked at, mentioning at least some key issues.

The proportion of variable capital (simplified 'labour costs') of the total capital is decreasing (Marx looked at this under the heading of the tendency of the organic composition of capital to fall, actually something that Adam Smith also mentioned before him). This is of course a contradictory process, since the 'servicialisation' suggests a different pattern: services are inherently labour intensive and the potential for rationalisation in these areas is limited.[5] In any case, the 'inner colonialisation', already mentioned especially by Rosa Luxemburg *(see also page 56 f.)*, is not least also a matter of a further shift in the composition of capital. In addition to the proportions of constant and variable capital we have to look more closely at the qualitative character of the respective shares. Latest at this point it becomes clear that the analyses, originally looking at industrial capitalism, needsto be revisited, although not completely revised.

Another socio-economic aspect, being result and cause of processes, needs to be taken into account. Looking at the development of income we can generally assume a tendency of an increase of the overall amount of variable capital, at the same time however a decrease of income (notwithstanding the enormous growth of wealth, i.e., the concentration of high income in the hands of a 'relevant minority of the population').[6] Going hand in hand with this we see a shift in the structure of qualification as the actual qualification is lowering.[7] This means also that the availability of employment on the upper echelons of the qualification

[3] German history gives apt evidence for how dramatic such differences can be – and even if the historical process had always been complex and contradictory, an important facet of the truth is that German fascism was mainly a result of the representatives of heavy industry, whereas light industry favoured at least initially other internal and external strategies. We cannot really compare the current situation with that of the 1920s and then 1930s/40s only in very limited ways, but we are surely standing at a crossroads where the decision has to be taken going beyond looking for mechanisms that are limited by solely aiming on overcoming the current crisis.

[4] In fact, this can be understood if we emphasise that it is capital and not the individual capitalist.

[5] When looking at the wider context, as the debate about quality of development (see the paragraph Prosperity as Happiness, 175), it is interesting that rationalisation changes always 'content' as well – often the provision of more or different services is a consequence of shortcomings of earlier service provision.

[6] The reference to the one percent is a little bit misleading: though the statement is in principle correct, i.e., correct in highlighting that there is only a small number exercising control it lets us overlook that the number of rich and very rich people is increasing. Still, even if taken literally we find actually a frightening figure here too. According to an OXFAM-issue briefing titled Wealth: Having It All And Wanting More (Oxfam, 2015) '[i]n 2014, the richest 1% of people in the world owned 48% of global wealth, leaving just 52% to be shared between the other 99% of adults on the planet.1 Almost all of that 52% is owned by those included in the richest 20%, leaving just 5.5% for the remaining 80% of people in the world. If this trend continues of an increasing wealth share to the richest, the top 1% will have more wealth than the remaining 99% of people in just two years, as shown on Figure 2, with the wealth share of the top 1% exceeding 50% by 2016.' (ibid.: 2)

[7] This is not necessarily reflected in the degree obtained.

scale decreases. In other words, there are more jobs at the lower end of the qualification ladder than in the middle or at the top. – It is in socio-economic terms important to see this as both cause and effect, since the formal qualification actually increases. The latter is part of the commodification of education, which results in a decreasing meaning of the ever-higher formal levels of education: in substantial terms the focus is on skill-acquisition. Another aspect in this context is the increasing demand for higher formal qualifications. Furthermore it is in socio-economic terms important that these shifts are closely linked with issues of gender and migration. In this light it can surely be viewed with mixed feelings that women are in certain areas winners of an overall negative development. In other words: the worsening of the overall situation appears to be an improvement for those who are traditionally already marginalised. Though is wrong to say that the rising tide lifts all boats, it is correct to say that one feels better if the boat is sinking than one does if one is thrown over board, left to fight (or sink) alone.[8]

The overall balance of the composition of capital in a global perspective is of fundamental importance. Put in a nutshell, we can say that global shifts changed the distinct patterns of international division of labour which was up to recently reasonably distinct: the rich global north standing against the poor global south. Today there is a tendency on a dual scale: It is still correct to speak of the rich global north and the poor global south.[9] However, at the very same time wealth and poverty in the north and in the south are emerging not least in qualitative terms in new ways *(see e.g., Draibe, 2010).* This is not simply a question of new inequalities; more important (and largely not analysed) is the fact that we are also facing a shift in the structure of capital. In simple terms: as far as the theory of centre and periphery was more than an analytical tool and reflected at least partly the distribution of the different departments across space,[10] we are today dealing with a system, that is characterised by a mix on both sides. This means that within national economies and also on the global scale some borders are blurring.

The shifts of *income* structures and *capital* structures are closely interwoven: the income gap is growing, and actually takes a form that resembles a pair of scissors with asymmetric blades; at the same time the capital structure appears in new forms:

- concentration and centralisation continue to increase;
- we see at the same time the emergence of an ‘entrepreneurial reserve army’, i.e., a ‘stable pool’ of small and medium-sized enterprises, which can be equally regarded internationally as foundation on which large enterprises establish their ‘empires’
- thirdly, a group of ‘new freelancers’ is emerging, itself divided into several sub-groups – a common feature is that their economic and life perspective is characterised by precarity and/or the fact that people belonging to this group lost the links to traditional forms of social integration and securitisation

[8] Corsi, Marcella, 2014: Economic Independence and the Position of Women on the Labour Market of the European Union; in: A new strategy for gender equality post 2015; Compilation of briefing notes - part I; Workshop 3.9.2014; PE 509.984; Directorate General for Internal Policies. Policy Department C: Citizens' Rights and Constitutional Affairs. Gender Equality; Brussels: European Parliament: 38-63; obvious for instance in figure 4, reproduced from Eurostat

[9] leaving aside that part of this global south is geographically located in the east.

[10] Department I: production of means of production; Department II: Production of consumables – so far we find this in the work of Marx’s classification; Department III, following Luxemburg: financial services; I think a Department IV should be added, this can be seen as non-mediating service

- finally, the group of the old small and medium entrepreneurs in very different positions remains an essential part of the overall structure.

Of course, the role of banks and more in general of the financial sector is significant: until recently a macroeconomic equilibrium, understood in very broad terms, had been possible by shifting costs in time and space – here banks played an important mediating role, maintaining at least the appearance of such equilibrium (one could use the metaphor of banks being the doors which kept light out of the darkroom). However, now, with the given excess money, which cannot be profitably invested in the productive sphere, the fact that money is needed for sustaining life and the opportunities of global speculation, the financial sector does not continue to be a facilitator. Instead we are dealing with a relatively autonomous sphere: the traded funds are neither centrally part of strategic industrial policies, nor do they secure financing of private households that would at least stimulate demand in the medium and long-term perspective.[11] – Now the finance sector is acting as shiny spotlight that makes the actual process of production disappear by the process of harsh blinding – the resulting picture equals the truth gained from spotlights directed into the eyes of any accused.

We see as well a massive shift in the sphere of consumption. Part of it is the increasing importance of loans needed to finance the consumption of private households. On the one hand this characterises the gradual preparation and factual emergence of financialisation. At the same time we see an underlying shift of major significance: wage labour is further decoupled from the social process. As much as the importance of the various departments of the overall economic process shifts towards the financial sector, the perspective of living and working shifts to a secondary level of securitisation: what had been initially a matter of financing consumption, is becoming increasingly a matter of circular (re)production.[12]

VARIETY WITHIN THE ONE CAPITALISM

Of course, many of these moments are not in themselves new, and it has to be noted as well that we are talking about tendencies, constituting a contradictory setting – this applies in national, regional and global perspectives. We may say that the new character emerges from the intensification of its elements – new is surely the more determined and overt character of the bonds. This intensification of the different aspects and the new dimensions of their interconnection represent a qualitative leap. It is essential that the previously existing conditions, establishing a seeming, at most temporary equilibrium, do not exist any longer. The supposed normality was clearly evidenced as exception – and the frequently feared or announced 'end of normal' can in some respect be also seen as return of normal.

[11] In this context it should not be overlooked that the end of Bretton Woods meant by and large the loss of control over monetary and fiscal policy. This means also a shift in the control, the 'strong economies' loosing some of their power, the 'weak economies' gaining some control. However, this has to be qualified by emphasising that this shift is taken back again by imposed austerity commitments mean a return to violent dispossession.

[12] This is also known as rat race: working in order to pay the debt that had to do be made due to insufficient income, and once starting the race it ends with not having time anymore to spend the money which is still not sufficient anyway. ... Sure, this is a complex process and the circle continues, the speed increases and while the private debt rate increases the margin for building up savings is naturally narrowing.

In whichever way we take it, the crucial point is that some fundamentals of capitalism cannot be taken for granted anymore. Four crucially changed aspects are about the meaning of the nation state, the centrality of production of tangible goods, the sole claim of enterprise-based employment and the meaning of full-time employment as dominant form of securing livelihood. With the erosion of these foundation stones, the following developments are of immediate relevance: (i) the end of spatial and temporal asynchrony – thus limiting the possibility of externalising problems; (ii) a relatively high degree of alignment of the composition of capital, thus limiting the *'Varieties of Capitalism' (see box),* and (iii) the perverting pressure on the ratio of the different types of income: mass incomes are not sufficient enough to ensure demand that is sufficient to guarantee profit;[13] high incomes are beyond a threshold that can be converted into purchasing power; at the same time this particular section of the high income earners grows immeasurably, indicating that these private incomes increased in tendency to the extent to which capital is converted into private assets, i.e., de-capitalised – as capital in strictu sensu it cannot be maintained anymore and takes the form of private wealth; finally, especially the lower and even middle income is coming under further pressure, because the lack of resources, needed to make ends meet – we see the need to 'enhance' low incomes by (small) loans – at most this warrants some short-term mitigation of the pressure, however increasing the weight of insufficiency in the medium- and long term perspective, not least by the accumulation of loans and interest that have to be paid (back).

Excursus: Varieties of Capitalism – distracting from debating fundamentals

Daniel Buhr and Rolf Frankenberger summarise the idea of *varieties of capitalism,* being brought into the wider debate by Peter Hall and David Soskice into the discussion *(s. Hall/Soskice (eds.) 2001),* by stating, 'that different institutional frameworks of the political economy result in systematic differences in the development of corporate strategies.*' (Buhr/Frankenberger, 2014; here: 64).* They name five prominent areas: industrial relations, organisation of education and training, corporate finance and relations with financiers, regulating the relationship between enterprises and integration of the workforce *(s. ibid.).* And they criticise that 'conditions the statutory-institutional framework and the influence of the state coming from business, going beyond the five spheres they mention' *(ibid.)* are not considered.

When it comes to the analysis of the crisis and the evaluation of further development two aspects are of particular importance:

After the first, most disturbing but 'focussed' shock, triggered by the collapse of Lehman Brothers, the situation became increasingly confused. What was initially seen as tip of the iceberg named 'general global crisis', gained increasingly different faces, which were often discussed independent from each other or even seen as contradicting each other. Many of these facets had been legitimately highlighted as crisis factors: financial crisis; US banking crisis with global impact; state budget crises; lack of profitable investment spheres etc. pp. Undoubtedly many important points were made in the various analyses of particular aspects, however, in their isolation often arriving at false conclusions – for the latter we may look at

[13] The core of the process is of course not securing demand as matter of satisfying needs.

the mismanagement in some EU member states: though there had been surely mistakes made in EU-member states (e.g., unsubstantiated tax policy in Ireland, the early capital and wealth flight from Greece and diverse speculative investment projects in Spain), it is misleading to blame 'the countries' for the consequences of earlier policies favouring national minorities.

PARADISE LOST – EMERGING UNCERTAINTIES AMONGST THE RULING CLASSES

Sure, there was and still is the simple statement that '[i]n the season of resurrection, it's fitting that he's with us once again — bearded, prophetic, moralistic, promising to exalt the humble and cast down the mighty from their thrones. Yes, that's right: Karl Marx is back from the dead.' *(Douthat, 2014)* So indeed: 'Marx is alive' *(Günther, 2008)* and the suggestion that 'Karl Marx is going mainstream' *(Jeffries, 2012)* is not really surprising. But leaving the more 'popular discourse' aside, it is of particular interest that the general optimism of mainstream economics and the recourse to the traditional means was indeed increasingly under pressure, although this did not result in a principle transformation of thinking. Still, it is worthwhile to highlight some recent examples.

1. The International Monetary Fund (IMF) highlighted in an article, published in January 2014, the dramatic worsening of inequality, stating 'that high income inequality can be detrimental to achieving macroeconomic stability and growth.' *(IMF, 2014)*
2. According to the Spiegel-Magazin (see Böcking/Dieckmann, 2014) the leading German economic research institutes left to some degree the otherwise prevailing affirmative role behind, positioning themselves against policies of strict fiscal consolidation.
3. We find as well a critique from another side, namely as review from Lagarde who can surely be seen as somebody who represents an organisation that carries a lot of responsibility for the political and economic failures – before the proceedings of the annual meeting of the International Monetary Fund and the World Bank' Lagarde (underlined) that public investment are in the longer term also good for state budgets. This could be not only growth-friendly but also friendly when it comes to the development of debt. 'The members have to show a much higher financial commitment, directed towards increasing today's growth and tomorrow's growth potential' Lagarde writes in a strategy paper on the occasion of the event.' *(Spiegel Online, October 09, 2014)*

Of course, one must wonder, reading in the same article that 'Finance minister Schäuble (...) intends to look at the possibility of strengthening German investments.' *(Ibid.)*

4. Already a short time earlier we can read that the Monetary Fund outlines the danger of a new economic crisis – the following reasons were given:

> Instead of the anticipated recovery after years of economic crisis, there is a risk of stagnation within the Eurozone. This year the single currency area will grow by 0.8 percent, and in the coming year by 1.3 percent. Both values had been significantly reduced.
>
> Also geopolitical crises such as the one in Ukraine and in the Middle East could cause economic damage far beyond the affected areas, for instance due to rising energy prices.
>
> A possible overheating of the financial markets is also a risk. The currently high market prices would not reflect the actual fragility of the economic recovery.
>
> Despite low interest rates we face especially in large economies underinvestment and too little is done for the demand.
>
> Moreover, there are numerous nations in urgent need for structural reforms. The late effects of the great recession about six years ago were more persistent than previously thought. (Spiegel Online, 2014 October, 7)

5. Of course, all this is not the a political assessment by the editors of the editorial board; in fact it reflects the discussions at various levels. Thus we see that Marco Buti, EU Director General of the DG Economic and Financial Affairs, welcomes the reader of the European Economic Forecast for Fall 2014 already in the editorial with the clear and disillusioned statement: 'After just a year of moderate growth, the momentum of the EU economy began to slow in spring 2014. In the second half of this year, GDP growth in the EU is set to be very modest, while in the euro area it will almost stagnate. Among the largest euro area Member States, we see growth increasing in Spain where unemployment remains very high, growth coming to a stop in Germany after a very strong first quarter, protracted stagnation in France, and contraction in Italy.' *(Burti, 2014)*
6. Even if it is indeed too late and the damage is immense; and even if we have known it for a long time and also talked about it, it is remarkable that the self-criticism has reached (only) now the top decision makers:

> The International Monetary Fund's internal watchdog has criticised the fund's call for austerity in 2010. The move reopens a heated debate among policy makers about the merit of raising taxes and cutting public spending after the financial crisis.
>
> In a review of the IMF's response, the independent evaluation office praised the fund's international lending role but attacked the policy advice it gave in 2010 for governments to start cutting their budget deficits. (Harding, 2014)

One has to add: reached once again, for such late insight is by no means historically unique – and thus we may tend to push them aside. Still, it is more appropriate to turn it into something positive. The underlying investigation is certainly sufficiently supported by the results shown by various evaluations. The report stems form the Independent Evaluation Office of the International Monetary Fund *(Independent Evaluation Office of the International Monetary Fund, 2014).*

Actually these and various other comments on the economic development, economic policy and economics and the indicated uncertainty should not be underestimated. Although currently the spectre that haunts Europe seems to be largely invisible, the devil can be found around every corner. In addition to these more high-level, high-visible discussions, mentioned before, these uncertainties and ambiguities can also be seen if one looks at the discussions during the *Informal Meeting of the Labour Ministers in Milan*[14] or the conference in Rome, aiming on *Unlocking the Potential of the Social Economy for EU Growth;*[15] the discussions during fora such as the fourth Sorrento meeting *'Mezzogiorni d'Europa e Mediterraneo – Transizioni Sostenibili e Visioni Rovesciate' (Sorrento 7-8 November 2014);*[16] or the debate on *'Un Nouveau Départ Pour L'investissement'* in early December 2014 , looking at *'Les clés de l'Investissement d'une relance.'*[17] All these reflect at least uncertainties on sides that had been earlier certain of the status quo.

Concrete Blocks As Barriers

Hans-Werner Sinn, when looking at the 'sacred cow' of the growth-oriented competition, is clear: 'Competition is one of the fundamental conditions under which the invisible hand can act whereas monopolies and oligopolies exploit consumers and restrict output.' *(Sinn, 2014)*

And to ensure this supposedly indispensible competition, even government intervention is accepted from this unexpected angle:

> The left uses the term neoliberalism as an insult. They are starting from the assumption that neo-liberalism is the doctrine of deregulation of the economy and the suggestion of the state as night watchman. This is not correct. ... It comes from Alexander Rüstow, who declared in 1932 at the annual meeting of the Association for Social Policy the end of the old liberalism and demanded a new liberalism with a strong state that would establish a solid legal framework for enterprises. (ibid.)

In fact, keeping the old terminology and concepts, prevents the recognition of the largely changed conditions as well as the orientation on new perspectives. In addition to the various truncations of the analysis – picking one, though often important aspect and not thinking about the relational character – it is obvious that the simple indication, credited to Einstein, namely that '[w]e cannot solve our problems with the same thinking we used when we created them',[18] was simply ignored. The following aspects are central.

Hegemonic Systems

Debates are again and again focussing on securing national competitiveness and growth. However, adherence to the principle of nationality should be even for conservative economic policy making obsolete. Globalisation has today, both with regard to the extent and with regard to the character, reached a status that requires a shift in thinking. 'We Are One World'

---

[14] http://italia2014.eu/media/1376/plenary-ii-social-economy.pdf; 18/11/14
[15] http://socialeconomyrome.it; 18/11/14
[16] http://www.bancheimprese.it/it/sorrento-meeting-2014/sorrento-meeting-2014.html; 18/11/14
[17] http://www.confrontations.org/images/confrontations/Conference/2014/Invitation-Assises-europeennes-du-long-terme.pdf; 18/11/14
[18] http://www.brainyquote.com/quotes/quotes/a/alberteins121993.html#92cjUybIiqGItXLc.99 - 09/01/15

is no longer just an ideological demand for the recognition of the rights of other countries and regions and their people; rather, we have reached a stage of interconnection that requires to rethink the concept of globalization: the conventionally associated understanding of centre-periphery relations has become in some ways questionable, even though massive imbalances continue to exist. In addition to the realignment of the world order we have to take serious the growing importance of semi-peripheries, the development towards a unipolar world, at the same time the tendencies towards a multi-polar world, the orientation on regionalisation as a mechanism discarding efforts of domination, the attempts to establish counter-hegemonies etc.

Growth-Mania

Growth is apparently still unquestionable. This is true even if one includes the following considerations: The report[19] presented in 2009 by the *Commission on the Measurement of Economic Performance and Social Progress*[20] *received major* recognition in the media. It emphasised the need to consider not only the growth rates of GDP, but also other factors, namely 'quality of life' and 'sustainable development and environment', as matters of societal progress. These were *placed alongside* the 'classical topic' GDP. This means that the important question of a fundamental reformulation of the problem suggested by the title 'Measuring economic performance and social progress' was not even clearly stated. Growth performance is seen as independent and as such GDP growth remains unquestioned and universal. This is not only defined as conditio sine qua non, but moreover it is understood as core of the entire social fabric. Given the persisting overproduction and overheating of innovations – adding new products without adding use value – this may be in two ways surprising: on the one hand it is remarkable that despite the alleged slowdown the output of production is still rather high;[21] in addition, it has to be asked if such generalised orientation on growth is compatible with a claimed orientation towards environmental protection, sustainability and happiness. – By and large these discussions are currently approached in very narrow ways. This applies as well to discussions within the left, clearly visible when we look at the hype about the EU plans: growth, without any further qualification, is still seen as nearly the only possible and universal answer to the crisis, as it allows defining practical measures that can help people to overcome the immediate plights. – Alternatives are seen, but remain underdeveloped within the debates on immediate actions.

In any case this confirms two things: the crisis did by no means reach an end – as said, at this stage it is even acknowledged by the usually faithful beacons of hope of the current economic system; and there will be no way out of the crisis as long as the mechanisms that are causing the crisis are not challenged: the reduction of complex political and economic relationships on an understanding of society as mechanical settings, suggesting that consumption equals prosperity and welfare, and require more growth of commodity production, more wage labour, then quasi-automatically resulting in more prosperity. – Both,

[19] http://www.stiglitz-sen-fitoussi.fr/documents/rapport_anglais.pdf; 14/11/14

[20] http://www.stiglitz-sen-fitoussi.fr/en/index.htm; 14/11/14

[21] see e.g., the figures compiled at Wikipedia: Gross world product http://en.wikipedia.org/wiki/Gross_world_product, 22/01/15

the suggested chain and the suggested perception of wealth and prosperity are not fully grasped in this understanding.

Disembedding

Having talked earlier about a new, structural dimension of the crisis refers essentially to the disintegration of the different areas: Economy and economic activities are established as relationships of capital and as such this social construct, based in power relations, is forcefully separated from the metabolic process between humans and nature. This aims arguably on enforcing an artificial equilibrium (which, in fact, has never been reached); as such it is removed from complex social relations and vice versa: social relations are redefined and only valued as much and as long as they are geared to maintaining this utilitarian circularity. One may say that since capitalist relations are social relations, their current socio-political form expresses a complete perversion. Even competition takes on a new, further perverted form and it transforms itself into infantilised, egomaniac, autistic, irrational *hominem solvi.*

Karl Polanyi pointed to the complex relationship. According to him we are not simply dealing with a predominance of specific economic interests. Rather, it is a relational process, i.e., the totality of political-economic orientations and the redefined foundations:

> The market pattern, on the other hand, being related to a peculiar motive of its own, the motive of truck or barter, is capable of creating a specific institution, namely, the market. Ultimately, that is why the control of the economic system by the market is of overwhelming consequence to the whole organization of society: it means no less than the running of society as an adjunct to the market. Instead of economy being embedded in social relations, social relations are embedded in the economic system. (Polanyi, 1944: 57)

This is another grasp of the tendency of changing the meaning of the economic process itself. Hand in hand with the shift from reciprocity and redistribution to the dominance of market exchange as mentioned by Polanyi we find a redefinition of the market itself. At the outset of market development, in particular in pre-capitalist forms, we find demand and goods and services only emerging as 'reply'; however, the emergence of capitalist markets and market societies means the inversion of this relationship. The very principle of capitalist accumulation – and this is the only driving force of such market economy – is generating profit: Neither the luxury consumption nor the general improvement of living conditions stood at the centre – at most they had been 'necessary by-product'. Consumption was, in other words, necessary condition but by now means sufficient. It has to be noted that necessary does not mean that this consumption has to take place locally – rather the opposite is advantageous: Export implies the possibility of keeping wages (i.e., potential purchasing power) low. In short, capitalist accumulation is the basis for a multi-layered development:

- shifting production from demand- to supply orientation;
- shifting from local to external demand, i.e., the emphasis of foreign trade;
- shifting from the production of consumer goods to services-provision;

- along with this the increasing inner colonialisation, i.e., the increasing penetration of both the work process and the process of consumption by the requirements of capitalist realisation *(Marx, 1867passim).*

Taken together, this means that the process of accumulation is increasingly reflexive – financialisation is its blatant expression. Production – and the association with real life, i.e., real people's needs and problems in everyday's life – appears nearly as a disruption of the self-referentiality of the financial system.[22] Pleas for a green growth, a new green deal, social investment, local currencies, etc. are against this background highly problematic as long as the basic patterns of capitalist accumulation are not questioned.

Karl Marx highlights the connection between the political-economic dimension, the juridical control over the entire process of work/labour and the socio-cultural dimension[23] by looking at the complexity needed when discussing the right to work, stating 'the first clumsy formula … transformed into the *droit à l'assistence,* the right to public relief … The right to work is, in the bourgeois sense, an absurdity, … . … [B]ehind the right to work stands the power over capital; behind the power over capital, the appropriation of the means of production, their subjection to the associated working class and, therefore, the abolition of wage labour, of capital and of their mutual relations.' *(Marx, 1850: 77 f.; see also page 60 of the present publication)* In other words, the question of dis-embedding and re-embedding is not least a question of fully establishing the character of work/labour as social movement.

Prosperity As Happiness

Despite – and because of – these extreme shifts and divides as evidenced by massive inequality, retrenchment, restructuration and undersupply, we are facing a debate on lifestyle issues, well-being, quality of life and the like.

It has to be emphasised that these debates are in many instances moving into dangerous directions: as much as growth is in other perspectives over-emphasised, we see now a tendency to portray life as matter of good luck, suggesting that we all possess enough and the decision about lifestyle would be simply a private affair (even if of societal meaning and importance), depending on subjective sensations and free personal decisions. This notion does not change if it is linked to some calls for a new enlightenment, for a wider understanding of rationality. It is equally problematic to refer to an 'imperial mode of living' *(Brand/Wissen)* without embedding its definition into a thoroughly understood framework referring to the objective development of the productive forces.

It is important to recognise that the process of disembedding and attempts of re-embedding are a matter that concerns the entire economic process and economic relations, not only the question of consumption, calling for responsibility as cure.[24] As much as relations of capital are social relationships, such move would only mean to 'reverse' the perspective, resulting in the definition of social relationships as relations of capital. This is not the topic of

[22] On the question of Reality becoming unreal see e.g., Herrmann, Peter 2014 b

[23] The latter frequently coming up today under the heading of a work-life-balance, clearly showing the dis-embeddedness of capitalist wage labour

[24] We may say the latter is a matter of the 'superstructure' – not in the understanding of the juxtaposition of basis and superstructure but as matter of a multi-level analysis of the process of production and accumulation.

the present contribution.[25] One frequently neglected factor is the availability and utilisation of the existing productive forces. Therefore it would be wrong to emphasise a 'new modesty' and refer to the necessity of changing values and expectations. It is important to think about ways of exploiting the existing potentials in different ways. This refers in particular to the following societal pillars:

- socio-technical potentials, i.e., the use of technical means as part of the entire process of metabolism with nature
- redistribution of the existing private wealth in favour of lower and middle income groups
- societal redistribution of wealth from the private to the public sphere, not least as a matter of tax policies, and subsequently the production of public goods[26]
- opening new legal dimensions, namely the right to self-determination of production, going hand in hand with the quest for full responsibility[27]
- finally control of banks, especially emphasising the commitment to sustainability and the link to the productive process.[28]

Again, the following has to be considered: all these aspects have to be taken in conjunction, they have to be understood in the overall context. An important building block for further reflections is the four-in-one perspective, as it had been presented by Frigga Haug. It involves 'to redefine time, wealth and labour in new ways'.

> The aim is not to magically arrive at new labour, but to redistribute the work that does exist. This means that we move towards distributing all human activities – the sphere of employment, the sphere of reproduction, the sphere of personal development and the sphere of politics – between all individuals in the same proportions. We start from a hypothetically working day of 16 hours. Within this time span, the four dimensions of life have ideally four hours each. This is not mechanically designed, measured with a stopwatch, but serves as a sort of guideline. (Haug, 2014: 33)

Crisis Management or 'Abolition of the Crisis'

The perversion of both, the crisis and the limited readiness to search for ways forward that are more radical can be shown by a pun:

---

[25] It should be noted that this is different to the common understanding of social capital.

[26] Public infrastructure and public services are only part of it.

[27] Brandt talks about the assertion of the 3rd generation of human rights *(Brand, 2014: 11)*, but fails to recognise that this 3rd generation is defined as matter of protection; however, a new development requires developing rights that are guaranteeing effective self-determination. Discussions in Latin America about the relations between humans and nature/natural environment and the rights of indigenous people are of great interest – it is in many instances about new dimensions that cannot be fully grasped within the framework of the commonly accepted Western legal doctrine.

[28] It remains an open question what this exactly means – not least because an important part of current banking business would disappear; it is also necessary to develop an understanding of financial policy and banking business that is not oriented on growth.

> Excessive cheap production and low fare trade, being a major feature of quantitative growth strategies are established on the strategies of sheep advertising and 'low fair production'. (Herrmann, 2014 a, with reference to: Carvajal, 2006)

The obsession with growth is currently especially strong in a weird marriage with an odd search for alternatives to mainstream development. Looking at some examples may show the 'perversion of contradictions' or better to say the 'dialectic of perversion': people are speaking of 'green policies' when sheep are used as advertisement medium to boost growth – even if the mentioned New York Times article is referring to advertising for hotels and using sheep as advertising medium, one still has to think of the environmental impact of travelling. Also, taking other areas, alleged justice and redistribution goes hand in hand with actual exclusion: supermarkets with low-cost products such as Lidl, Aldi, Primark secure mass-consumption, but this is subject to hugely problematic working conditions, low wages and thus also a matter of exclusion.[29]

Of course, such discussions are not really about Primark or individual companies although managements should surely not be allowed to escape from their responsibility. However, the core of the issue is the overall structure which is still geared towards avoiding to address the real issues. For instance the chief executive of the Association of the German Textile and Fashion Industry, Uwe Mazura, argues as follows:

> Essentially, it is a question of sustainably improving the social and environmental conditions of the international clothing industry and the lives of people in the producing countries. We explicitly share this goal. However, only very few factories of the medium-sized German enterprises own the production plants themselves and utilise instead local producers for the fabrication of clothes. We are not the employer, but only purchasers. (Siems, 2014)

Displaying exploitation as a kind of social benefit or welfare measure, in this case: providing employment locally in the countries in question, is nothing new. Indeed, we should not be surprised that stores such as Lidl and Tchibo are today to a considerable degree part of such trade, though their claimed 'core business' is grocery and coffee respectively. Also, the working conditions in these shops and the related warehouses should not be forgotten, even if a company like KiK textiles advertises itself as an environment protection and welfare agency – certainly a field that goes beyond corporate identity.

This is surely important for developing thinking about prospects further, not least as it highlights the need to think about new patterns of legitimation.

---

[29] The following quote provides apt evidence:

The specialist in research of trade, Weber, sees this in a similar way. He says 'The price battle is being carried out on the backs of the producers'. And it is done in a way that is not acceptable. 'The working conditions are desastrous.' For instance in Bangladesh, the main country for deliveries for the low-price segment, (female) workers have to work seven days per week, twelve hours per day, Weber reports.

Without holidays and without maternity leave. The fact that the fashion is shifting major production capacities from China to Bangladesh has according to the expert mainly two reasons: Firstly, there the wages are ten times lower than in the People's Republic; on the other hand there are no significant environmental regulations. Especially the latter is shamelessly utilised.

(Bohmann / Dierig / Seidel, 2012; see also Herrmann, 2012)

A further important issue is in this context the question of street traders.

The shift of the economy towards service-provision and subsequently the inner colonialisation reaching a qualitatively new stage, as it had been mentionend earlier, is also hugely important. Though this is at first glance simply a matter of furthering capitalist hegemony, we can see on the other hand the existing potential. Probably it is not much of an exaggeration to conclude that we reached with this crisis indeed the stage which Marx characterised already:

> At a certain stage of their development, the material productive forces of society come into conflict with the existing relations of production or - this merely expresses the same thin in legal terms – with the property relations within the framework of which they have operated hitherto. From forms of development of the productive forces these relations turn into their fetters. Then begins an epoch of social revolution. ... No social formation is ever destroyed before all the productive forces for which it is sufficient have been developed, and new superior relations of production never replace older ones before the material conditions for their existence have matured within the framework of the old society. (Marx 1859: 263)

Such conclusion is not least justified if we consider the problematique which I discussed elsewhere under the heading 'Capitalism in One Country?' *(see Peter Herrmann/Vyacheslav Bobkov, forthcoming: Economy of Difference and Differentiation; in: Herrmann Peter/Bobkov, Vyacheslav (Eds.): Precarity – Searching for a New Theoretical and Empirical Perspective).* Nearly reaching the state of complete global hegemony, the various factors that stabilised as main push and main pull factors global capitalist development during the preceding stages of a globally contested system (the definitive bipolar world, system competition, the conditions that allowed development of underdevelopment etc.) ceased to exist *(see also page 56f. in this volume and also the contribution* World Systems Theory and Theory of Social Quality as Proposal for a Methodology for Rethinking a World in Crisis and Transformation*).*

Thus, we may look at the current situation and development in a more positive way, unfolding the roots of future development. We are at a point that requires not primarily a moral shift; instead these questions have to be understood within the context of objective changes of the foundations. This allows to see the turning point arising from the development of the productive forces and the relative stage and forms of socialisation. The underlying theory consists of several elements – on the one hand we can detect a set of potentials, on the other hand we face a set of necessities – both sides will be briefly presented below.

The basic thesis is that we are dealing with a serious aggravation of the development and moreover with the development model itself – the term crisis in its common understanding is too weak to actually grasp this. This situation leads to real threats of internal and external violence and social emergencies. It also means that especially the left – taken in a wide understanding – has to elaborate and highlight the existing possibilities. The orientation on the status quo ante, i.e., the unconditional restoration of the status quo ante means to hope for solutions from those conditions that are the very causes of the present difficulties.

Potentials

We find both, nationally and regionally and increasingly globally enormous wealth – often not fully recognised behind the enormous inequality and the pressing needs to deal with adjoined extreme poverty: private and corporate assets are frequently reaching beyond the resources of national budgets of even large countries *(see also Footnote 61)* – in short: *'There is enough for all.'*

Concepts and debates on well-being, buen vivir, quality of life and many similar notions and concepts are ultimately an expression of major dissatisfaction with the material abundance and the unilateral utilitarian, individualistic and 'materialistic' orientation of life, reflecting the words that are attributed to Einstein: 'Not everything that counts can be counted, and not everything that can be counted counts'; dissatisfaction is also increasingly virulent on the side of those who are marginalised, seeing themselves immediately confronted with prosperity, thus experiencing face-to-face the secular paradise lost; in any case, this is not simply a matter of subjective dissatisfaction and perceived futility; it is as well the experience of lack of any power over the own life. Much is possible but there is little we can do: *'All are frustrated.'*

Capabilities, human resources, social capital, vivir buen, good life, happiness research, social quality and other suggestions of assessment of progress by more and other ways than measuring progress by looking at narrowly understood indicators of economic performance, are as well showing that the objective foundation of the economic process itself has changed. Alienation became an objective factor: control over the metabolism with nature escapes increasingly human action, and definitely the action of individuals while at the same time sociability is undermined; enormous potentials of control given by modern IT-technologies revert into the accumulation of unintended consequences of individual action – earlier the end of normal and the new normal are mentioned and part of it can b e seen in this development of the also technically defined destruction of the foundations of social existence, understood as matter of production and reproduction of people's daily life. In this context the current level of development – technologically, in terms of resource relations, social, informational etc. – allows to break with traditional forms of division of labour: in many areas this is indeed already happening. Interestingly we find such new modes to a large extent in form of small and limited activities (namely as niches representing alternative lifestyles or also in some recreational activities); however, such moments can also be found as 'nests' settling within frameworks of traditional production: the supposed paradisical working conditions variously described for google[30] are even remarkable if only half of these images hold true. In short, *'all going together can easily mobilise the resources and potentials for the needed change'*. – All this shows that we are not talking about 'moderation' or looking for a 'different logic', but that we have to establish conditions that follow a different logic, and consequently it is about producing a different logic; public goods are one of the important examples; the social economy is another example. In short: *'The existing resources are sufficient to move much further than simply securing existence.'*

We also have to investigate more closely the productive potentials – actually globally working time is considerably reduced,[31] at the same time the extremely unequal distribution

[30] Of course, caution is needed as not all reports provide a positive light.
[31] Not in the understanding as presented by Hartz, 2001

both in national and regional as well as global perspective is a manifest problem – in short, *'We have more than is needed to satisfy just the needs and wants of a small group.'*

Necessities

The rupture between self-referential 'economic' systems and metabolism with nature creates increasingly limits. Whether we refer to expected catastrophes', see shock doctrines at work or use a more moderate analysis, it is obvious that we reached the limits of this type of economy: One might speak of limits to growth, as limits arising from a quasi-hostile confrontation between man and environment, or as limits of human beings to cope with further alienation from themselves – on the concrete level the respective interpretations open different perspectives, but the one conclusion they have in common is simple: we need urgently a fundamental reorientation.

Intergenerational equity and justice is another field, which urgently needs to be addressed. Although it is important to acknowledge that solidarity as principle of societal organisation never existed undisputedly, we can say that today it simply does not exist at all, as far as we are looking at the material dimension. This is not (only) about having borrowed the world from our children, but also about the fact that pension systems, health care, education systems, etc. are structurally characterised by a short-term orientation, not offering financial or material perspectives for the future.

The erosion of peaceful global relations may remain within limits which make a new world war unlikely – although we should be aware that a global escalation is not completely unthinkable. In any case, there are countless acute conflicts recorded.[32] – In this context equally relevant are strives for re-regionalisation and renationalisation – there are surely different legitimate interpretations of these developments, very particular in every single case. But at the end, all these movements are an attempt to escape a 'perceived permanent conflict'. And they are an attempt to regain power and control. And as such they mark a complicated relationship between different hegemonies within and across borders of identity: nations against nations, religions against religions, ..., and again and again allowing the blurring of borders and the blurring of the underlying core class interests *(see e.g., Poulantzas, 1975).*

An increasingly urgent issue evolves around the so-called principle of governance, new approaches towards defining public and private, rights and obligations, formal and effective democratic rights etc. As burdensome and limited as many of the traditional patterns of political regulation are due to their rigidities, exclusiveness etc., it must also be seen that the suggested new and supposedly alternative governance- and stakeholder principles are by and large only an application of the ideology of economic management in the political sphere. In this light we face a massive threat on democratic and rights-based features of (bourgeois)

[32] For a short overviews

Among the total of 414 observed conflicts the political scientists see 45 highly violent conflicts, i.e., conflicts that are characterised by the widespread use of organised violence, and having serious consequences. Accoring to the experts, 20 of these conflicts can be classified as war – due to their level of intensity. This high level had been also reached in 2011; the 'Conflict Barometer 2012' reports 18 as number of wars.

Although Europe was not affected by war during the last year, the conflict researchers observed an increase in the number of violent crises. The scientists saw the opposition conflict in Ukraine as well as newly emerging conflicts in Greece as examples.

(Heidelberg Institute for International Conflict Research, 2014; translation P.H.)

democracy, which may then turn into patterns of paternalist politics and polities, politics and policies and charitability: Bill and Melinda Gates and Bertelsmann are just two examples, the German Foundation even more remarkable, as it stands for untold political influence in the 'spirit of new community building'. Only clear political and legal frameworks can act against the arbitrariness of such New Princedoms *(see Herrmann, 2010/2012).*

FIRST THINGS FIRST ... WHAT SHOULD BE PLACED ON THE AGENDA?

1. ***Investments*** are high on the agenda as growth is here and now top priority, in the short run an immediate necessity as part of the solution of problems emerging from the crisis. It is important to ensure from the outset public control and most importantly it must be guaranteed that private investment is not executed by way of re-establishing the same structures that caused the crisis: investment securing high profit margins in the short run, preventing the development of a long-term-oriented, sustainable infrastructure. This means not least that with the emphasis of growth the emphasis of quality of investment for a changed quality of the developmental process is essential.
2. ***Large-scale investments*** are required, but this does not mean that these are individually large investments. Especially small 'projects' may be able to change qualitatively the ways in which existing means of production are used. This can be about urban and regional development, conversion of production and the change of the organisation of production, such as the (re-)development of cooperatives.[33]
3. ***Public infrastructure*** has to be set high on the agenda: education, child care, health care ... – these are areas that need to be expanded, but also qualitatively expanded under public control – better-educated political and business leaders could certainly have saved us a lot of trouble.
4. ***Monitoring of the financial sector and in particular banks*** is required, and it must go far beyond regulation of speculation control. A central moment is the 're-embedding' of financial transactions in the entirety of production and reproduction of human existence. Banking transactions relating to the financing of enterprises and households are in this case immediately effected. Responsibility by political public bodies and by cooperatives needs to be strengthened – but not by a voluntary act but on the basis of real and full socialisation of the control over the means of production.[34]
5. In addition to the management of banks and the banking system the ***creation of a new monetary system*** and a ***new mechanisms for international coordination*** are an urgent priority.[35]
6. It is urgent to finally take the global dimension seriously – this means to understand the ***'world market' as matter of a global society*** – one step towards such perspective

[33] However, whether micro-finance provides an opportunity is highly contested.

[34] This links immediately into the point that had been mentioned before, namely investment in small projects etc.

[35] If a new Bretton Woods (http://www.avvenire.it/Politica/Pagine/appello-dei-340-economisti-al-premier.aspx; 20.11.149) can be a solution or if it is necessary to find another way is a question that needs urgently to be addressed.

may be the introduction of global budgeting, allowing to identify all costs and profits.

7. It has to be elaborated if new budgeting and accounting procedures can be developed, allowing the ***exclusion of 'social investment' from the calculation of debt.***
8. ***Democracy*** has to be understood as matter of economic policy. It is important to ***(re-)establish worker participation on the enterprise level*** – this requires spaces that are free from pressure and ensure, for example, that relocation of production cannot be used as means of extortion. International work councils are one crucially important element.
9. ***Reduction of Working Hours*** is an urgent issue – but it must not be mechanically used; instead it has to be embedded in a well-elaborated societal framework as suggested by Haug's *Four-in-One-perspective* – as such it reflects the objective conditions and necessities of a complex process of socialisation.
10. ***Redistribution now*** is the last, though also the most important requirement – various means are available, and we need not least a fiscal policy, which (i) answers the need of radical redistribution and (ii) which can be used as means of regulation. Responsible means also that it requires democratic control – local budgets are one mechanism that has to be examined in this light.

REFERENCES

Böcking, David/Dieckmann, Florian, 2014, Oktober 9: Ökonomen drängen auf Abkehr vom Spardiktat. Ausgeglichener Haushalt 2015; in SpiegelOnline; http://www.spiegel.de/wirtschaft/soziales/haushalt-2015-forscher-kritisieren-sparkurs-von-schaeuble-a-996269-druck.html; 03/11/14 11:27.

Bohmann, C./Dierig, C./Seidel, H., 2012, August 8: Der Trick mit den Billig-T-Shirts aus Irland. Modekette „Primark"; in: *Die Welt*; http://www.welt.de/108480170; http://www.welt.de/wirtschaft/article108480170/Der-Trick-mit-den-Billig-T-Shirts-aus-Irland.html; 16.11.14.

Brand, Ulrich, 2014: Sozial-ökologische Transformation als gesellschaftspolitisches Projekt; in: Kurswechsel 2/2014: 7-18; hier: 11 [nach dem Korrekturbogen, dankenswerterweise vom Autor vor Veröffentlichung verfügbar gemacht.

Buhr, Daniel/Frankenberger, Rolf, 2014: Spielarten des inkorporierten Kapitalismus; ; in: Nölke, Andreas/May, Christian/Claar, Simone (Eds.): *Die großen Schwellenländer.* Ursachen und Folgen ihres Aufstiegs in der Weltwirtschaft; Wiesbaden: Springer VS: 61-84.

Burti, Marco, 2014: Editorial; in: European Commission; DG for Economic and Financial Affairs, 2014: European Economic Forecast. Autumn 2014; Brussels: European Union; ix; http://ec.europa.eu/economy_finance/publications/

Carvajal, Doreen, 2006, April 24th: Advertiser counts on Sheep to Pull Eyes Over Wool; in: *New York Times*; http://www.nytimes.com/2006/04/24/world/europe/24sheep.html; 08.12.14).

Douthat, Ross, 2014: Marx Rises Again; in: *The New York Times*; Sunday Review; April 19, 2014; http://www.nytimes.com/2014/04/20/opinion/sunday/douthat-marx-rises-again.html, 1/22/15.

Draibe, Sônia Miriam, 2010: The Debate on Social Cohesion in Latin America: orogons, issues and some lessons from successful experiences; in: Zupi, M./Estruch Puertas, E. (Eds.), 2010: Challenges of Social Cohesion in Times of Crisis: Euro-Latin American Dialogue; Madrid: Editorial Complutense: 171-202.

Günther, Franziska, 2008: Marx lebt; in: Zeit online; 24. October 2008 19:33 Uhr; http://www.zeit.de/online/2008/44/marx-revival, 1/22/15.

Hall, Peter/Soskice, David (eds.) 2001: Varieties of Capitalism: The Institutional Foundations of Comparative Advantage. Oxford: Oxford University press.

Harding, Robin, 2014, November 4: International Monetary Fund criticised over support for austerity; http://www.ft.com/cms/s/0/4b077fd0-6431-11e4-8ade-00144feabdc0.html; November 4, 2014.

Hartz, Peter (2001), Job Revolution. Wie wir neue Arbeitsplätze gewinnen können, Frankfurt: Frankfurter Allgemeine Zeitung BuchVerlag.

Haug, Frigga, 2014: Zeit, Wohlstand und Arbeit neu definieren; in: Zeitwohlstand. wie wir anders arbeiten, nachhaltig wirtschaften und besser leben; Hrsg.: Konzeptwerk Neue Ökonomie e.V.; München: oekom verlag, Gesellschaft für ökologische Kommunikation mbH: 27-38.

Heidelberger Institut für Internationale Konfliktforschung, 2014, Februar 25: Konfliktbarometer: Zahl der Kriege 2013 erneut auf dem Höchststand; http://www.uni-heidelberg.de/presse/meldungen/2014/m20140225_konfliktbarometer.html; 20.11.14; für den Gesamtbericht: http://hiik.de/de/downloads/data/downloads_2013/Conflict Barometer2013.pdf; 20.11.14.

Herrmann, Peter, 2010/2012: Prolegomena. Encore Citizenship – Revisiting or Redefining?; in: Herrmann, Peter (ed.): *World's New Princedoms*. Critical Remarks on Claimed Alternatives by New Life; Amsterdam: Rozenberg Publishers, 2010 and Bremen/Oxford: academicpress, 2012: 17-76/9-80

Herrmann, Peter, 2012 (6/18): ‚Global Nationalism': Economics – Social Quality - Measurement; http://williamthompsonucc.wordpress.com/2012/06/18/global-nationalism-economics-social-quality-measurement/; 20.11.2014

Herrmann, Peter, 2014 (a): Strengthening the European Social Model by Going Beyond; http://williamthompsonucc.wordpress.com/2014/10/31/strengthening-the-european-social-model-by-going-beyond/; 16.11.14.

Herrmann, Peter, 2014 (b): Where are we going?; http://williamthompsonucc.wordpress.com/2014/12/07/where-are-we-going/; 08.12.14.

Herrmann, Peter/Bobkov, Vyacheslav, forthcoming: Economy of Difference and Differentiation (working title); in: Herrmann Peter/Bobkov, Vyacheslav (Eds.): *Precarity – Searching for a New Theoretical and Empirical Perspective*.

IMF, 2014, January, 23: Fiscal Policy and Income Inequality. Approved by Sanjeev Gupta; Washington: IMF: 4; http://www.imf.org/external/np/pp/eng/2014/012314.pdf; 19/11/14.

Independent Evaluation Office of the International Monetary Fund, 2014 (October, 08*): IMF Response to the Financial and Economic Crisis: An IEO Assessment*; http://www.ieo-imf.org/ieo/files/completedevaluations/Full%20Text%20of%20the%20Main%20Report.pdf; 16/11/14

Jeffries, Stuart, 2012: Why Marxism is on the rise again; in: The Guardian, Wednesday 4 July 2012 20.00 BST; http://www.theguardian.com/world/2012/jul/04/the-return-of-marxism, 1/22/15.

Mahnkopf, Birgit, 2010: Leitbilder auf dem Weg au der neoliberalen Sackgasse; Hrsg.: Institut Solidarische Moderne, Schriftenreihe Denkanstöße; http://www.solidarische-moderne.de/de/article/43.leitbilder-auf-dem-weg-aus-der-neoliberlaien-sackgasse.html; 08.12.14.

Marx, Karl, 1850: The Class Struggles in France. 1848 to 1850; in: Karl Marx. Frederick Engels. *Collected Works*. Volume 10: Marx and Engels 1849-1851; London: Lawrence&Wishart: 45-145.

Marx, Karl, 1859: A Contribution to the Critique of Political Economy. Part One; in: Karl Marx/Frederick Engels. *Collected Works*. Volume 29. Marx: 1857-1861; London: Lawrence&Wishart, 1987: 257-417

Marx, Karl, 1887: Capital, Volume I [German first edition 1867]; in: Karl Marx. Frederick Engels. *Collected Works*. Volume 35; London: Lawrence & Wishart, 1996.

Oxfam: Having It All And Wanting More; OXFAM issue briefing; January 2015 - http://www.oxfam.org/sites/www.oxfam.org/files/file_attachments/ib-wealth-having-all-wanting-more-190115-en.pdf - 19.01.15.

Polanyi, Karl, 1944: The G*reat Transformation: The Political and Economic Origins of Our Time;* Boston: Beacon Press, 1957.

Poulantzas, Nicos, 1975: Classes in Contemporary Capitalism [original: Les Classes Sociales dans le Capitalisme Aujourd'hui; Paris: Editions du Seuil, 1974]; Translated by David Fernbach; London: NLB.

Siems, Dorothea, 2014, Oktober 13: "Ein Boykott wäre eine humanitäre Katastrophe." Textilproduktion; Interview; http://www.welt.de/133195196; http://www.welt.de/wirtschaft/article133195196/Ein-Boykott-waere-eine-humanitaere-Katastrophe.html; 16.11.14

Sinn, Hans-Werner, 2014, November 1: Sie sind wie Spürhunde. Ignorante Kritik an Ökonomen; in: Süddeutsche Zeitung; http://www.sueddeutsche.de/wirtschaft/kritik-an-oekonomen-der-grosse-irrtum-1.2198333; 10/11/2014.

SpiegelOnline, 2014, Oktober 7: IWF warnt vor neuer Weltwirtschaftskrise. Schwaches Wachstum; http://www.spiegel.de/wirtschaft/soziales/iwf-warnt-vor-weltwirtschaftskrise-a-995868-druck.html; 03/11/14.

SpiegelOnline, Oktober, 09, 2014: Lagarde ruft nach staatlichen Investitionen. IWF-Chefin; http://www.spiegel.de/wirtschaft/soziales/iwf-chefin-lagarde-draengt-mitgliedslaender-zu-hoeheren-investitionen-a-996351-druck.html; 03/11/14.

DEDICATION CONTINUED

As said, when I heard about the Massacre against Charlie Hebdo, I was working in the library of *l'école française de Rome.* Located in the Palazzo Farnese, one of the monuments, representating the ancient regime, accommodating the treasures of the liberal thinking of the educated classes and … and next to the *Campo de' Fiori* – the daily local market, the piazza where so many tourists enjoy being emerged in this spot of local civility, vivacity and veniality – and where the monument of Giordano Bruno overlooks the square: surely by many ignored, and surely by many others seen as a historical figure, a figure of history, a figure of the past whose meaning for today, and whose ongoing significance is easily forgotten.

A man who was fighting long before the emergence of those values which emerged later with the elevation of the halved modernity – and he was fighting in their favour because he asked for acceptance for these values also when they appeared to be inconvenient. We may say: he was fighting for the second half of modernity even if the first had not yet been reached – and for this he was ready to die.

http://upload.wikimedia.org/wikipedia/commons/0/00/Giordano_Bruno_Campo_dei_Fiori.jpg-09/01/15

INDEX

G

H

I

K

L

M

N

P

R

S

U

V

W